Illicit Trade

Misuse of E-Commerce for Trade in Counterfeits

This work is published under the responsibility of the Secretary-General of the OECD and the Executive Director of the EUIPO. The opinions expressed and arguments employed herein do not necessarily reflect the official views of the OECD Members or the European Union Intellectual Property Office.

This document, as well as any data and map included herein, are without prejudice to the status of or sovereignty over any territory, to the delimitation of international frontiers and boundaries and to the name of any territory, city or area.

Please cite this publication as:
OECD/EUIPO (2021), *Misuse of E-Commerce for Trade in Counterfeits*, Illicit Trade, OECD Publishing, Paris, *https://doi.org/10.1787/1c04a64e-en*.

ISBN 978-92-64-61712-4 (print)
ISBN 978-92-64-58876-9 (pdf)
ISBN 978-92-64-82113-2 (HTML)
ISBN 978-92-64-52769-0 (epub)

Illicit Trade
ISSN 2617-5827 (print)
ISSN 2617-5835 (online)

European Union
ISBN:
978-92-9156-302-9 (print)
978-92-9156-303-6 (pdf)
Catalogue number:
TB-01-21-341-EN-C (print)
TB-01-21-341-EN-N (pdf)

Photo credits: Cover © By PopTika.

Corrigenda to publications may be found on line at: *www.oecd.org/about/publishing/corrigenda.htm*.
© OECD and EUIPO 2021

The use of this work, whether digital or print, is governed by the Terms and Conditions to be found at *http://www.oecd.org/termsandconditions*.

Preface

Trade in counterfeit and pirated goods poses a serious and growing risk to economic growth, undermining good governance, the rule of law and citizens' trust in government. Illicit trade networks tend to misuse many modern solutions, including e-commerce, a modern tool offering numerous advantages for consumers and businesses. The COVID-19 pandemic has accelerated illicit trade and the degree of abuse of the online environment.

Policy makers need solid empirical evidence to take action against this threat. To meet this need, the OECD and the EU Intellectual Property Office (EUIPO) have joined forces to carry out a series of analytical studies. The results have been published in a set of reports that gauge illicit trade in counterfeit and pirated goods.

We are pleased to see this new evidence that sheds additional light on the abuse of e-commerce facilities in trade in counterfeit and pirated goods. We are confident that the results will assist policy makers in shaping effective solutions to combat and deter this risk, and to promote clean trade in the post-COVID recovery.

Christian Archambeau,
Executive Director,
EUIPO

Elsa Pilichowski
Director,
OECD, Public Governance Directorate

Foreword

Illicit trade in fake goods is a significant and growing threat in a globalised and innovation-driven economy. It has damaging effects on governance, innovation, and, ultimately, economic growth.

In recent years, the OECD and the EU Intellectual Property Office (EUIPO) have been gathering evidence on various aspects of this trade. The results have been published in a set of factual reports, starting with *Trade in Counterfeit and Pirated Goods: Mapping the Economic Impact* (2016). The results have been deepened, expanded and updated in subsequent reports, including *Misuse of Small Parcels for Trade in Counterfeit Goods: Facts and Trends* (2018), *Trends in Trade in Counterfeit and Pirated Goods* (2019) and *Global Trade in Fakes: A Worrying Threat* (2021). Throughout the reports, the issue of abuse of e-commerce by networks of trade in counterfeit goods was constantly present. The misuse of the online environment has become particularly worrying during the COVID-19 pandemic, with law enforcement detecting increasing volumes of various e-crimes.

This report uses a tailored statistical methodology to gauge the degree of abuse of the online environment in the context of trade in counterfeit goods. It also provides highlights of government actions and industry initiatives to counter this risk. Such analysis is critical, not only for a better understanding of this threat, but also for developing effective governance responses to support post-COVID recovery.

The results are a cause for concern. E-commerce is becoming the main platform for some illicit products, including fake and substandard medicines, test kits, protective equipment and other COVID-19-related goods. Counterfeiters misuse modern logistical solutions such as e-commerce, and exploit market gaps lacking effective enforcement standards, such as postal services. Today, e-commerce is becoming a platform for buying counterfeits by consumers in developed countries, and in some countries seizures of counterfeits related to e-commerce purchases constitute the vast majority of all seizures of fakes. The COVID-19 pandemic has intensified the problem: criminal networks have reacted very quickly to the crisis and adapted their strategies to take advantage of the shifting landscape.

This study was carried out under the auspices of the OECD's Task Force on Countering Illicit Trade, which focuses on evidence-based research and advanced analytics to assist policy makers in mapping and understanding the vulnerabilities exploited by illicit trade.

Acknowledgements

This report was prepared by the OECD Public Governance Directorate (GOV), under the leadership of Elsa Pilichowski, Director, and Martin Forst, Head of the Governance Reviews and Partnerships Division, together with the European Union Intellectual Property Office (EUIPO), under the leadership of Christian Archambeau, Executive Director, and Paul Maier, Director of the European Observatory on Infringements of Intellectual Property Rights.

This study was conducted under the auspices of the OECD Task Force on Countering Illicit Trade (TF-CIT). The study was shared with other OECD committees with relevant expertise in the area of trade, regulatory policy, public sector integrity and digital economy policy.

The report was prepared by Piotr Stryszowski, Senior Economist and Morgane Gaudiau, Economist at the OECD Directorate for Public Governance jointly with Michał Kazimierczak, Economist at the European Observatory on Infringements of Intellectual Property Rights of the EUIPO and Nathan Wajsman, Chief Economist, EUIPO. Peter Avery and Jean-Paul Rebillard provided significant inputs. The authors wish to thank the OECD experts who provided valuable knowledge and insights: Julio Bacio Terracino, Alessandro Bellantoni and Nick Malyshev from the OECD Public Governance Directorate, and Silvia Sorescu from the OECD Trade Directorate.

Andrea Uhrhammer and Ciara Muller provided editorial and production support.

The database on customs seizures was provided by the World Customs Organization (WCO) and supplemented with regional data submitted by the European Commission's Directorate-General for Taxation and Customs Union, the US Customs and Border Protection Agency and the US Immigration and Customs Enforcement. The authors express their gratitude for the data and for the valuable support of these institutions.

Table of contents

Preface   3

Foreword   4

Acknowledgements   5

Executive Summary   9

1 Introduction   11
Background   11
Scope of the study   12
References   13

2 E-commerce: The economic landscape   17
Introduction   17
Market trends   17
Industry structure   19
Consumers   21
Risks of counterfeits offered on-line   22
References   31

3 The trade in fakes: A first glance   36
Data   36
E-commerce and trade in fakes at a first glance   38
Focus on small parcels   43
References   49

4 Trade in fakes and e-commerce: Focus on the EU   53
Seizures related to online transactions   53
Transport modes   55
Provenance economies   58
Types of fakes purchased online   60

5 Governance frameworks   63
Government-led measures   63
Actions of online platforms   68
References   70

6 Concluding remarks 74
References 76

Tables

Table 2.1. World e-commerce in 2019 18
Table 2.2. Retail sales in selected economies, 2018-20 18
Table 2.3. Cross-border B2C e-commerce sales of the top 10 merchandise exporters, 2019 19
Table 2.4. Largest B2C e-commerce companies, 2020 20
Table 2.5. Number of online shoppers worldwide (in billion of persons), 2017-19 22
Table 2.6. Operation Pangea 2008-2018 24
Table 2.7. Processing of letters and parcels by postal authorities in recent years 30

Figures

Figure 3.1. Proxy of online purchases (in log) and number of customs seizures (in log), 2019 39
Figure 3.2. Proxy of online purchases (in log) and value of customs seizures (in log), 2019 39
Figure 3.3. Proxy of online purchase (in log) and number of global customs seizures (in log), 2017 40
Figure 3.4. Proxy of online purchase (in log) and value of global customs seizures (in log), 2017 41
Figure 3.5. E-commerce Index and number of global customs seizures (in log), 2019 42
Figure 3.6. E-commerce Index and value of global customs seizures (in log), 2019 43
Figure 3.7. Proxy of online purchase in European countries (in log) and number of customs seizures by mail and EC (in log) 44
Figure 3.8. Proxy of online purchase in European countries (in log) and the value of customs seizures by mail and EC (in log) 45
Figure 3.9. Proxy of online purchase (in log) and number of global customs seizures by mail & express courier 46
Figure 3.10. Proxy of online purchase (in log) and number of global customs seizures by mail & express courier 47
Figure 3.11. E-commerce Index and number of global customs seizures (in log) 48
Figure 3.12. E-commerce Index and value of global customs seizures (in log) 49
Figure 4.1. Distribution of detentions between online sales and detentions not related to online sales 54
Figure 4.2. Distribution of value of seizures between online sales and detentions not related to online sales 54
Figure 4.3. Distribution of detentions between transport modes 55
Figure 4.4. Share of detentions related to online sales within each transport mode (online and not online=100%) 56
Figure 4.5. Distribution of value of counterfeit goods between transport modes 57
Figure 4.6. Provenance countries of seizures not related to online sales (share of detentions) 58
Figure 4.7. Provenance countries of seizures related to online sales (share of detentions) 58
Figure 4.8. Provenance countries of seizures not related to online sales (value of seized goods) 59
Figure 4.9. Provenance countries of seizures related to online sales (value of seized goods) 59
Figure 4.10. Distribution of number of detentions not related to online sales between product categories 60
Figure 4.11. Distribution of number of detentions related to online sales between product categories 60
Figure 4.12. Share of detentions related to online sales by good category (by number of detentions) 61
Figure 4.13. Share of detentions related to online sales by good category (by value of seized articles) 62

Boxes

Box 2.1. Big data 21
Box 2.2. Consumer deception vs. knowing demand for fakes 23
Box 2.3. EU Consumer Rights Directive 26
Box 2.4. EU General Data Protection Regulation (GDPR) 28
Box 5.1. Governance measures in Belgium 64

Follow OECD Publications on:

 http://twitter.com/OECD_Pubs

 http://www.facebook.com/OECDPublications

 http://www.linkedin.com/groups/OECD-Publications-4645871

 http://www.youtube.com/oecdilibrary

 http://www.oecd.org/oecddirect/

Executive Summary

This study presents a quantitative review of the abuse of e-commerce to facilitate trade in counterfeits. In recent years, e-commerce has been expanding rapidly as consumers have become increasingly confident in ordering goods and services online.

The number of businesses engaged in business to consumer (B2C) e-commerce is constantly growing. Between 2018 and 2020, online retail sales, a subset of the B2C total, rose by 41% in major economies, compared to less than a 1% rise in total retail sales. The increase was fuelled by the COVID-19 pandemic, as consumers ordered online during lockdowns and to avoid frequenting shops. During the pandemic, the online environment also became a more popular target for illicit trade. Cyber law enforcement reported increasing volumes of various e-crimes, including offerings of illicit goods, among them fake and substandard medicines, test kits and other COVID-19-related goods.

The growing popularity of e-commerce has been used by counterfeiters, who are increasingly using e-commerce to sell fake items to consumers, some of whom purchase the items thinking they are genuine, while others actively seek out low-priced fakes.

The links between e-commerce and illicit trade in counterfeits are supported by quantitative analysis, which examines the relationship between e-commerce and the number and value of customs seizures of counterfeit goods during 2017-19. The analysis finds that the relationship becomes stronger when indicators of illicit trade in counterfeits misusing small parcels are included; this suggests that illicit goods purchased via e-commerce are often shipped via small parcels, using postal services in particular.

A case study of the European Union, which collects data on detentions of counterfeits linked to e-commerce, provides further insights into the situation. The data show that 91% of detentions of counterfeits linked to e-commerce involved the postal service. In contrast, the post was involved in only 45% of the detentions of counterfeits not linked to e-commerce. In terms of value, the data show that 82% of detentions linked to e-commerce involved the post, compared to only 9% for other counterfeits. With respect to provenance, the sources of counterfeits were similar for those linked to e-commerce and those that were not; however, China's share of the total was higher in the case of counterfeits linked to e-commerce (76% vs. 46% of total number of detentions).

The EU detentions of counterfeits linked to e-commerce included a broad range of products, led by footwear (34% of total detentions), clothing (17%), perfumes and cosmetics (10%), leather articles (9%), electrical machinery and equipment (7%), toys (6%) and watches (5%).

Counterfeit sellers have flourished on e-commerce markets, as it is relatively easy to set up sites that sell counterfeit items. Moreover, they continue to find new ways to infiltrate trusted platforms with their counterfeit products. Law enforcement is actively engaged in identifying and closing down fraudulent sites and working with major platform operators and brand owners to target sales of counterfeits, but the problem remains significant and is growing.

The difficulty of intercepting counterfeits has been exacerbated by the means through which products ordered via e-commerce are shipped. Counterfeiters have been adept at exploiting weaknesses in distribution channels to facilitate their illicit operations. In the case of e-commerce, this is done largely through the post. There is concern that postal authorities and customs are not well positioned to screen shipments of small parcels and letter packets for counterfeits. They have limited capacity to detect counterfeits traded internationally, as the shipments of mailed counterfeit items are intermingled with billions of legitimately traded items.

Governments have taken a range of actions to combat online sales of counterfeit items, including establishing agreements with stakeholders that are designed to strengthen co-operation, and enhanced efforts to detect and act against websites that sell counterfeit items.

For example, in the European Union, the European Commission was behind the drafting and implementation of a Memorandum of Understanding (MoU) among platforms, brand owners and other stakeholders, to promote good practices in the fight against the sale of counterfeit goods over the Internet. In the United States, the government spearheaded the creation of an Electronic Commerce Working Group, which brought major online platforms together to collaborate and co-operate on ways to combat counterfeiters selling on their platforms. In Australia, the government is developing a mechanism that allows consumers to identify sellers of legitimate products, by linking authorised sellers of specified brands to the government's trademark registry. Moreover, in the European Union and the United States, legislation and directives are being considered that, if adopted, would establish new frameworks for combatting e-commerce crime, including trade in illicit goods.

Major platform operators have developed multifaceted approaches to combat sales of counterfeit products on their platforms. Their efforts include measures and mechanisms involving third-party sellers, consumers, brand owners and law enforcement, as well as the development and deployment of strategies to proactively detect and move against counterfeits. The ability of platforms to adequately vet third-party sellers has, however, proven to be challenging, and efforts are constantly being made to improve the mechanisms for identifying and disciplining parties selling counterfeit items.

The analysis presented in this report demonstrates that the misuse by counterfeiters of online markets is very dynamic. Further investigation into how these dynamics evolve is needed, both at the industry level and through case studies. Further work should take the more granular aspects of the dynamic changes into account, while focusing on improving responses to emerging challenges, by identifying and promoting effective policies and practices.

1 Introduction

Background

Globalisation, policies for improving trade facilitation and the rising economic importance of intellectual assets are important drivers of economic growth. These intangible assets in the global trade context have shifted the attention of industry leaders and policymakers towards intellectual property (IP). For modern industries, IP is a key value generator and enabler of success in competitive markets. Meanwhile for policymakers, IP plays a crucial role in promoting innovation and driving sustained economic growth.

However, this rising importance of IP in the globalised world has created new opportunities for criminal networks to free ride on others' intellectual assets to pollute trade routes with counterfeits. The growing magnitude and broadened scope of counterfeiting, particularly in the context of trade, is seen as a significant economic threat that undermines innovation and hampers economic growth.

To provide policymakers with reliable empirical evidence on this threat, the Organisation for Economic Co-operation and Development (OECD) and the European Union Intellectual Property Office (EUIPO) joined forces to develop an understanding of the scale and magnitude of the IP infringement problem in international trade. The results are published in a series of reports that provide a general overview of this threat: Trade in Counterfeit and Pirated Goods: Mapping the Economic Impact (OECD/EUIPO, 2016[1]), Mapping the Real Routes of Trade in Fake Goods (OECD/EUIPO, 2017[2]), Trends in Trade in Counterfeit and Pirated Goods (OECD/EUIPO, 2019[3]) and Global Trade in Fakes: a Worrying Threat (OECD/EUIPO, 2021[4]).

Apart from these core reports, further studies have deepened our understanding on specific aspects of trade in counterfeit goods. These include Trade in Counterfeit Goods and Free Trade Zones: Evidence from Recent Trends (OECD/EUIPO, 2018[5]); Why Do Countries Export Fakes? (OECD/EUIPO, 2018[6]); Misuse of Small Parcels for Trade in Counterfeit Goods (OECD/EUIPO, 2018[7]); Trade in Counterfeit Pharmaceutical Goods (OECD/EUIPO, 2020[8]) and Misuse of Containerized Maritime Transport in Counterfeit Trade (OCDE/EUIPO, 2021[9]).

Altogether, these reports provide robust evidence of the significant volume of counterfeiting and piracy in global trade networks. In addition, they document the threat IP infringement poses to business efficiency and consumer well-being worldwide.

The existing literature has refocused policy attention towards combating counterfeit trade and piracy. This has been paralleled by increased efforts by the private sector to raise awareness of this global threat.

In addition, several recent developments could affect the counterfeit trade landscape. One key trend is the boom in trade in small parcels, which has been boosted by the COVID-19 pandemic. Furthermore, the lockdowns and border closures the on-going sanitary crisis has created – and will continue to create – have greatly impacted illicit trade in counterfeit goods. The effects of these developments occur through several direct and indirect transmission channels by shifting consumer demand, changing priorities in customs controls and re-shaping trade routes.

In recent years, counterfeit trade conducted through e-commerce platforms has played an increasingly important role in shaping illicit trade. E-commerce is also associated with trade in small parcels, so counterfeiting in e-commerce influences counterfeiting in trade in small parcels as well.

The purpose of this report is to provide policymakers with updated information on the links between illicit trade and e-commerce. The report provides measures comparing the frequency of online purchases with the number and value of global customs seizures shipped by mail, express courier (EC), and other conveyance methods. This methodology is used with a new set of world data on seizures of counterfeit and pirated goods and data on e-commerce which leads to a set of objectives and a robust illustration of economy- and industry-specific patterns in the trade of counterfeits.

The quantitative analysis in this report predates the COVID-19 pandemic. The pandemic has impacted both licit trade and the trade in counterfeit goods. While some initial effects on counterfeiting having already been observed, the longer-term impact is expected to emerge more gradually. Given the fast pace of change, a precise quantitative analysis of these effects has not yet been possible. Nevertheless, discussions with law enforcement officials and industry representatives, along with monitoring ongoing law enforcement actions, have shown that the main impact thus far has been an accelerated transition to e-commerce, with a boom in offers of counterfeits online. With consumers being forced to move to the internet, they are more motivated to use e-commerce platforms for their shopping needs. This has presented new opportunities for illicit actors to exploit e-commerce marketplaces and has likely contributed to growing levels of counterfeiting and piracy conducted online (OECD, 2020[10]); (OECD, 2020[11]) (UNICRI, 2020[12]).

Scope of the study

This analysis refers to two phenomena: counterfeiting and piracy and e-commerce.

Counterfeiting and piracy are terms used to describe a range of illicit activities related to the infringement of intellectual property rights (IPRs). Following the (OECD, 2008[13]), (OECD/EUIPO, 2016[1]) (OECD/EUIPO, 2019[3]) and (OECD/EUIPO, 2021[4]) studies, this report refers to the definitions as described in the World Trade Organization (WTO) Agreement on Trade-Related Aspects of Intellectual Property Rights (TRIPS Agreement). Consequently, this report focuses primarily on the infringement of copyright, trademarks, design rights and patents. The term counterfeit used in this report refers to tangible goods that infringe trademarks, design rights or patents, and the term pirated describes tangible goods that infringe copyright.

Three relevant aspects should be kept in mind in this context:

- This wording is used for the purpose of this report only and does not constitute any definition outside its scope. In particular, this study does not include intangible infringements, such as online piracy or infringements of other IPRs.
- Substandard, adulterated or mislabelled products, such as pharmaceuticals, that do not violate a trademark, patent or design right, for example, and replacement automotive oil filters and head lamps that are made by firms other than the original equipment manufacturer (OEM) (provided the replacement parts do not violate a patent, trademark or design right) are beyond the scope of this study.
- This study largely draws on statistical data on counterfeiting and piracy, which due to their nature are incomplete and limited. Consequently, the quantitative results presented in this study illustrate only certain parts of counterfeiting and piracy. Despite this, the methodological apparatus was tailored to the available dataset to ensure the conclusions are clear and based on fact.

In addition, defining e-commerce is a challenging tasks. The understanding of e-commerce is not universal, and the usage of the term varies in different contexts. For instance, the Eurostat manual definition differs from the US Census Bureau definition since the United States considers sales negotiated on extranets, email, and mobile devices (m-commerce) as e-commerce whereas Eurostat does not. Similar discrepancies exist between almost all organizations so it is important to underscore that the underlying data in this report comes from distinct sources that use slightly different definitions of e-commerce.

It is important to highlight that this report does not introduce any new definition of e-commerce, rather it uses the working description used in other similar OECD reports. This report looks at e-commerce as the sale or purchase of goods or services, conducted over computer networks by methods specifically designed for the purpose of receiving or placing orders, in line with the OECD definition established in 2001 and revised in 2009.[1]

References

Amazon (2021), *Brand Protection Report*, https://assets.aboutamazon.com/96/a0/90f229d54c8cba5072b2c4e021f7/amz-brand-report.pdf. [41]

Andrenelli, A. (2019), "Electronic transmissions and international trade - shedding new light on the moratorium debate", *OECD Trade Policy Papers*, Vol. 233, https://doi.org/10.1787/57b50a4b-en. [16]

DHS (2020), *Combating Trafficking in Counterfeit and Pirated Goods*, US Department of Homeland Security, Washington, https://www.dhs.gov/sites/default/files/publications/20_0124_plcy_counterfeit-pirated-goods-report_01.pdf. [32]

eBay (2021), *2020 Global Transparency Report*, http://www.ebaymainstreet.com/sites/default/files/2021-05/2020-eBay-Global-Transparency-Report.pdf. [40]

EC (2017), *Overview of the functioning of the Memorandum of Understanding on the sale of counterfeit goods via the internet, SWD(2017) 430 final*, https://ec.europa.eu/docsroom/documents/26602. [30]

EC (2016), *Memorandum of Understanding: 21 June 2016, Ref. Ares(2016)3934515 26/07/2016*, European Commission, Brussels, https://ec.europa.eu/docsroom/documents/43321/attachments/2/translations/en/renditions/native. [29]

EC (2013), *Report from the Commission to the European Parliament and the Council on the Functioning of the Memorandum of Understanding on the Sale of Counterfeit Goods via the Internet, COM(2013), 209 final,*, European Commission, Brussels,, http://Ref. Ares(2016). [28]

EC (2020b), *Report on the functioning of the Memorandum of Understanding on the sale of Counterfeit Goods on the internet, SWD(2020) 166 final/2*, European Commission, Brussels, https://ec.europa.eu/docsroom/documents/42701. [27]

EUIPO (2021), *Monitoring and analysing social media in relation to IPR infringement Report*, https://euipo.europa.eu/tunnel-web/secure/webdav/guest/document_library/observatory/documents/reports/2021_Monitoring_and_analysing_social_media_in_relation_to_IPR_Infringement_Report/2021_Monitoring_and_analysing_social_media_in_relation_to_IPR_Infringem. [20]

EUIPO (2021), *New and existing trends in using social media for IP infringement activities and good practices to address them*, https://euipo.europa.eu/tunnel-web/secure/webdav/guest/document_library/observatory/documents/reports/2021_Social_Media/2021_Social_Media_Discussion_Paper_FullR_en.pdf. [19]

GCIG (2016), *One Internet, Centre for International Governance Innovation and Chatham House*, http://www.cigionline.org/documents/1045/gcig_final_report_-_with_cover.pdf. [39]

Goldberg, S. (2019), "Regulating Privacy Online: An Economic Evaluation of the GDPR", *SSRN Working Paper*, http://dx.doi.org/10.2139/ssrn.3421731. [21]

Group, I. (2020), *IP Crime and Enforcement Report*, IP Crime Group Secretariat, Concept House, Newport, https://assets.publishing.service.gov.uk/government/uploads/system/uploads/attachment_data/file/913644/ip-crime-report-2019-20.pdf. [31]

INTA (2020), *Addressing the Sale of Counterfeits on the Internet*, https://www.inta.org/wp-content/uploads/public-files/advocacy/committee-reports/Addressing_the_Sale_of_Counterfeits_on_the_Internet_June_2021_edit.pdf. [22]

OCDE/EUIPO (2021), *Misuse of Containerized Maritime Shipping in the Global Trade of Counterfeits*, Éditions OCDE, Paris,, https://doi.org/10.1787/e39d8939-en. [9]

OECD (2021), *COVID-19 vaccine and the Threat of Illicit Trade, Chair's Summary Note*, https://www.oecd.org/gov/illicit-trade/summary-note-covid-19-vaccine-and-the-threat-of-illicit-trade.pdf. [35]

OECD (2021), *Illicit trade: Discussions with stakeholders*, unpublished. [26]

OECD (2020), *Illicit Trade in a Time of Crisis. Chair's Summary Note*, https://www.oecd.org/gov/illicit-trade/oecd-webinar-illicit-trade-time-crisis-23-april.pdf. [10]

OECD (2020), *OECD Digital Economy Outlook 2020*, OECD Publishing, Paris, https://doi.org/10.1787/bb167041-en. [11]

OECD (2020), *Trade in Fake Medicines at the Time of the Covid-19 Pandemics. Chair's Summary Note*, https://www.oecd.org/gov/illicit-trade/oecd-fake-medicines-webinar-june-10-summary-note.pdf. [34]

OECD (2018), *Governance Frameworks to Counter Illicit Trade*, OECD Publishing, Paris,, https://doi.org/10.1787/9789264291652-en. [33]

OECD (2011), *OECD Council Recommendation on Principles for Internet Policy Making*, OECD, Paris, https://www.oecd.org/sti/ieconomy/49258588.pdf. [37]

OECD (2008), *The Economic Impact of Counterfeiting and Piracy*, Éditions OCDE, Paris, https://doi.org/10.1787/9789264045521-en. [13]

OECD (2016a), *Ministerial Declaration on the Digital Economy*, OECD, http://www.oecd.org/digital/Digital-Economy-Ministerial-Declaration-2016.pdf. [38]

OECD (2016b), *Recommendation of the Council on Consumer Protection in E-commerce*, OECD, Paris, https://legalinstruments.oecd.org/en/instruments/OECD-LEGAL-0422. [17]

OECD/EUIPO (2021), *Global Trade in Fakes: a Worrying Threat*, OECD Publishing, https://www.oecd.org/publications/global-trade-in-fakes-74c81154-en.htm. [4]

OECD/EUIPO (2020), *Trade in Counterfeit Pharmaceutical Products*, Illicit Trade, OECD Publishing, Paris, https://dx.doi.org/10.1787/a7c7e054-en. [8]

OECD/EUIPO (2019), *Trends in Trade in Counterfeit and Pirated Goods*, OECD Publishing, Paris,, https://doi.org/10.1787/g2g9f533-en. [3]

OECD/EUIPO (2018), *Misuse of Small Parcels for Trade in Counterfeit Goods: Facts and Trends*, OECD Publishing, Paris, https://doi.org/10.1787/9789264307858-en. [7]

OECD/EUIPO (2018), *Trade in Counterfeit Goods and Free Trade Zones: Evidence from Recent Trends*, OECD Publishing, Paris/EUIPO, Alicante, https://doi.org/10.1787/9789264289550-en. [5]

OECD/EUIPO (2018), *Why Do Countries Export Fakes?: The Role of Governance Frameworks, Enforcement and Socio-economic Factors*, OECD Publishing, Paris/EUIPO, Alicante, https://doi.org/10.1787/9789264302464-en. [6]

OECD/EUIPO (2017), *Mapping the Real Routes of Trade in Fake Goods, Illicit Trade*, OECD Publishing, Paris, https://doi.org/10.1787/9789264278349-en. [2]

OECD/EUIPO (2016), *Trade in Counterfeit and Pirated Goods: Mapping the Economic Impact, Illicit Trade*, OECD Publishing, Paris, https://doi.org/10.1787/9789264252653-en. [1]

Phaneuf, A. (2021), *Social Commerce 2021: Social media and Ecommerce Convergence Trends Brings Growth Opportunity for Brands, Insider Inc.*,, http://www.businessinsider.com/social-commerce-brand-trends-marketing-strategies. [18]

S. Goldberg, G. (2019), "Regulating Privacy Online: An Economic Evaluation of the GDPR", *SSRN Working Paper*, http://dx.doi.org/10.2139/ssrn.3421731. [42]

Sorescu, S. (2021), "Trade in the time of parcels", *OECD Trade Policy Papers*, Vol. 249, https://doi.org/10.1787/0faac348-en. [15]

Tian, H. (2018), *Bullet-proof payment processors*, https://ieeexplore.ieee.org/document/8376208. [23]

UNCTAD (2021), *Estimates of global e-commerce 2019 and preliminary assessment of COVID-19 impact on online retail 2020*, United Nations Conference on Trade and Development, Geneva, https://unctad.org/system/files/official-document/tn_unctad_ict4d18_en.pdf. [14]

UNICRI (2020), *"Cyber-crime during the COVID-19 Pandemic"*, http://www.unicri.it/news/cyber-crime-during-covid-19-pandemic. [12]

UPU (2020), *E-commerce Guide*, Universal Postal Union, Berne, https://www.upu.int/UPU/media/upu/publications/Final-November-update-UPU-E-Commerce-Guide_2020_EN.pdf. [25]

USPS (2020/21), *FY 2020 Annual Report to Congress*, United States Postal Service, https://about.usps.com/what/financials/annual-reports/fy2020.pdf. [24]

WCO (2020), *Illicit Trade Report 2019*, WCO, Brussels,, http://www.wcoomd.org/-/media/wco/public/global/pdf/topics/enforcement-and-compliance/activities-and-programmes/illicit-trade-report/itr_2019_en.pdf?db=web. [36]

Note

[1] OECD (2019), Unpacking E-commerce: Business Models, Trends and Policies, OECD Publishing, Paris, https://doi.org/10.1787/23561431-en.

2 E-commerce: The economic landscape

Introduction

This chapter assesses the current state of business-to-consumer (B2C) and consumer-to-consumer (C2C) e-commerce globally, describing: i) the magnitude and scope of online sales, ii) the structure of the industry, iii) how consumers are increasingly using e-commerce to purchase an ever-expanding range of goods and services, and iv) the threat of fake goods being offered online and some of the related key areas.

Market trends

The development of the Internet has served buyers and sellers of goods and services well, by greatly enhancing the efficiency of markets, via e-commerce.[1] Consumers, for example, can access a far broader range of products, from a larger number of suppliers, than was previously the case. And businesses can expand the reach of their operations in a highly cost-effective manner that has proven beneficial to large and smaller entities alike. The increased transparency of markets has at the same time enhanced competition, spurring innovation.

The e-commerce market has three main segments: business to business (B2B), which dominates the market, business to consumer (B2C), which has risen sharply in recent years and consumer to consumer (C2C) which covers the sale of products between individuals that are not treated as businesses.[2] In 2019, e-commerce was estimated at USD 26.7 trillion, which accounted for about 30% of world GDP (Table 2.1). The United States, Japan and China were the top 3 economies in terms of e-commerce sales accounting for close to 60% of the world total. The importance of e-commerce across economies varied significantly, ranging from 14% in the case of Germany, to 79% in the case of Korea. As indicated above, B2B transactions dominated the market, accounting for 82% of all e-commerce, including both sales over online market platforms and electronic data interchange transactions.

Table 2.1. World e-commerce in 2019

Billions of USD and percent

Economy	Total e-commerce sales	Share of world total (%)	Share of GDP (%)	B2B e-commerce		B2C e-commerce	
				Sales	% of total sales	Sales	% of total sales
United States	9,580	36	45	8,319	87	1,261	13
Japan	3,416	13	67	3,238	95	178	5
China	2,604	10	18	1,065	41	1,539	59
Korea	1,302	5	79	1,187	91	115	9
United Kingdom	885	3	31	633	72	251	28
France	785	3	29	669	85	116	15
Germany	524	2	14	493	94	111	21
Italy	431	2	22	396	92	35	8
Australia	347	1	25	325	94	21	6
Spain	344	1	25	280	81	64	19
Subtotal	20,218	76	36	16,526	82	3,691	18
Other	6,455	24	20	5,277	82	1,179	18
Grand total	26,673	100	30	21,803	82	4,870	18

Source: UNCTAD, 2021.

The B2C market has experienced continued, rapid growth in many economies in recent years. Table 2.2 shows how the situation has changed, with respect to online retail sales, which represent a subset of the B2C sales reported in Table 2.1. The overall increase in online retail sales of 41% between 2018 and 2020 contrasts with the 0,16 % increase in total retail sales. At a country level, all countries listed experienced growth in online sales exceeding 33%, with sales in Canada and Singapore doubling. Total retail sales, on the other hand, declined in five of the seven economies listed, rising by less than 2% in the remaining two. As a result the share of online retail sales to the total rose sharply in all the economies, increasing to more than 20% in three economies.

Of course these changes were also driven by the COVID-19 pandemics. Due to lockdowns, the online environment has become more intensely misused, and cyber law enforcement has reported staggering volumes of various e-crimes, including offerings of counterfeits and other illicit goods. During the pandemic e-commerce has become the main platform for illicit products, including fake and substandard medicines, test kits and other COVID-19-related goods.

Table 2.2. Retail sales in selected economies, 2018-20

Billions of USD and percent

Economy	Online retail sales (USD bn)			Total retail sales (USD bn)			Online share of total (%)		
	2018	2019	2020	2018	2019	2020	2018	2019	2020
Australia	13.5	14.4	22.9	239	229	242	5.6	6.3	9.4
Canada	13.9	16.5	28.1	467	462	452	3	3.6	6.2
China	1,060.40	1,233.60	1,414.30	5,755	5,957	5,681	18.4	20.7	24.9
Korea	76.8	84.3	104.4	423	406	403	18.2	20.8	25.9
Singapore	1.6	1.9	3.2	34	32	27	4.7	5.9	11.7
United Kingdom	84	89	130.6	565	564	560	14.9	15.8	23.3
United States	519.6	598	791.7	5,269	5,452	5,368	9.9	11	14
Total of above	1,770	2,038	2,495	12,752	13,102	12,773	14	16	19

Source: UNCTAD, 2021.

The recent rise in online activity is, however, part of a longer-term trend. In the United States, for example, B2C e-commerce shipments rose by 267%, compared to 85% in the case of B2B manufacturing shipments.[3] In the process, the share of e-commerce retail sales to the total rose from 3.6% in 2008 to 9.9% in 2018, and to as high as 15.2% in the fourth quarter of 2020; at the same time the share of B2B manufacturing online activity rose from 40% in 2008, to 67% in 2018. Moreover, in the United Kingdom, B2C retail sales surged during 2020 and into 2021, jumping from 4.9% in 2008, to 28% in 2020 and 33% during January-April 2021.[4] By the end of 2021, some 93% of UK Internet users are expected to have engaged in e-commerce (OECD, 2021). Surveys indicate that the shift to online purchases is likely to continue as some 60% of those surveyed expected their online purchases to continue at elevated levels following the pandemic.

The Internet provides an effective mechanism for engaging in B2C cross-border trade, which in 2019 amounted to USD 440 billion (UNCTAD, 2021). As shown in Table 2.3, cross border B2C e-commerce transactions represented 2.3% of world merchandise exports in that year. While their role was relatively small in some economies, it reached 8.2% on the case of the United Kingdom. The share of cross border transactions in total B2C transactions amounted to 9%, exceeding 10% in six of the top 10 merchandise exporters listed.

Table 2.3. Cross-border B2C e-commerce sales of the top 10 merchandise exporters, 2019

(Billions of USD and percent)

Economy	Sales (USD bn)	Share of total merchandise exports (%)	Share of total B2C (%)
China	105	4.2	6.8
United States	90	5.5	7.1
United Kingdom	38	8.2	15.2
Hong Kong, China	35	6.2	94.3
Japan	23	3.3	13.2
Germany	16	1.1	14.7
France	12	2.2	10.6
Korea	5	0.9	4.4
Italy	5	0.9	13.9
Netherlands	1	0.2	4.3
Total of above	332	3.4	9
World	440	2.3	9

Source: UNCTAD, 2021

Industry structure

Goods and services can be sold on the Internet via e-commerce by companies, organisations and individuals, regardless of their size. Individuals, for example, can set up store fronts easily, at low cost, as can small shops. The number of sites engaging in e-commerce is constantly changing as new players enter the market and others exit. There are currently 12 to 24 million e-commerce sites; most are small as less than one million sellers sell more than USD 1,000 per year.[5] The larger e-commerce companies are multi-billion dollar enterprises, headquartered principally in China or the United States (Table 2.4). The 13 largest sold goods and services valued at USD 2.9 trillion in 2019, which accounted for close to 60% of total B2C sales in that year.

Table 2.4. Largest B2C e-commerce companies, 2020

(Billions of USD)

Company	Headquarters	Gross merchandise volume		
		2018	2019	2020
Alibaba	China	866	954	1,145
Amazon	United States	344	417	575
JD.com	China	253	302	379
Pinduoduo	China	71	146	242
Shopify	Canada	41	61	120
eBay	United States	90	86	100
Meituan	China	43	57	71
Walmart	United States	25	37	64
Uber	United States	50	65	58
Rakuten	Japan	30	34	42
Expedia	United States	100	108	37
Booking Holdings	United States	93	96	35
Airbnb	United States	29	38	24
Total	--	2,035	2,401	2,892

Source: UNCTAD, 2021

As indicated above, there are various types of B2C e-commerce platforms. *Marketplace platforms*, such as Alibaba, Amazon or eBay, sell a broad range of products, which are offered for sale from internal stocks or by outside vendors. The platform operator is responsible for attracting potential customers, advertising offers and processing transactions; they may also take responsibility for shipping products to buyers. *Retail store platforms* are operated by brick-and-mortar businesses; they provide consumers with a means to shop for and purchase products, for pick-up or shipping. They may also offer products from third party vendors, serving, in this case, as a marketplace platform as well. Other types of platforms include those operated by companies that offer virtual products or services, and those operated by manufacturers interested in selling their branded products directly to consumers, such as Apple, Godiva, Gucci, Levi's, Tiffany and Nike.

In terms of trends, conventional firms and retailers are increasingly experimenting with online distribution channels, alongside their brick-and-mortar operations (OECD, 2020[11]). This includes smaller retailers that are trying to survive during the drop-off of sales in physical stores due to the pandemic. There are challenges however as leveraging the Internet, or other electronic networks, to integrate e-commerce into an existing firm-level business model often requires complementary investments. This can include supply-chain and fulfilment arrangements, as well as consolidated inventory systems. In general, however, e-commerce shows much promise for small and medium enterprises, provided they have the resources needed to establish and maintain their own websites or, alternatively, engage with e-commerce platforms. There is scope for significant expansion; in 2019, e-commerce accounted for 24% of economic turnover in large firms, but only 10% in small firms (OECD, 2020[11]).

Innovation is ongoing in e-commerce markets. For example, marketing on-line has greatly improved thank to the access to large volume of data that businesses can analyze on a day-to-day basis. This phenomenon is called big data (Box 2.1) and offers insights that lead to more effective marketing and, more generally, better strategic decision making Another example it the "click and collect" mechanism, which enables consumers to order and purchase online and then collect purchased items in a local brick-and-mortar store or another location, such as a locker (OECD, 2020[11]). This allows consumers to immediately purchase a good or service at a distance, but to save on shipping costs, delays and the inconveniences that may be associated with delivery. The "click-and-collect" mechanism enables firms to retain their centralized inventory system, while reducing the operational costs associated with physical brick-and-mortar stores. Furthermore, it enables them to acquire useful data about users. To the extent that click-and-collect mechanisms are located in a brick-and-mortar store, they may allow consumers to check quality and assess the colour, style and size of the product within the store itself prior to purchase. In addition, consumers can make returns in-store, which can increase their willingness to purchase online.

> ### Box 2.1. Big data
>
> The Internet not only provides an effective and efficient vehicle for selling goods and services, but it also provides businesses and consumers with new ways to interact, providing both parties with opportunities to improve market experiences. Consumers, for example, generate enormous amounts of commercial and personal information that can be harvested and used by businesses to focus advertising more effectively, and to tailor products to meet specific consumer needs and interests. On average 12% of businesses in the OECD employed "big data" analytics in 2017, and 33% among large firms (OECD, 2020[11]). Data-intensive technologies such as artificial intelligence (AI) and the Internet of things (IoT) can be used to provide consumers with greater choice and personalization of products. At the same time, widespread use of personal information can pose new risks to safety, privacy and security. Already in 2019, over 80% of OECD countries reported AI and big data analytics as a significant challenge to privacy and personal data protection. In response, governments are implementing policies to raise awareness about privacy and data protection issues; they are also seeking policy solutions to address digital security issues.

Some online businesses in the fashion/clothing sectors are innovating by including offline features to enable the sale of fit-critical goods and services online (OECD, 2020[11]). While an offline distribution channel may increase costs, it can increase the extensive margin of e-commerce by enabling new types of products to be sold online. Firms that sell heterogeneous or customized products like clothing may benefit from consumers' ability to physically inspect the product before purchase. For example, several online apparel retailers have opened brick-and-mortar stores that allow consumers to try on products before ordering them online.

Other firms are experimenting with online ordering mechanisms within or near brick-and-mortar stores (OECD, 2020[11]). After entering a store via a mobile application, consumers can select the products and then leave the store without a formal checkout.

Consumers

Internet use, of which e-commerce is but one aspect, has risen sharply (OECD, 2020[11]). In 2019, 70% to 95% of adults used the Internet in OECD countries and smartphones became the favoured device for Internet access. There are, however, disparities within age groups and education level. Some 58% of individuals aged 55-74 used the Internet frequently in 2019, which is up from 30% in 2010. On the other hand, nearly 95% of individuals aged 16-24 were daily Internet users.

Increased Internet use is also reflected in an expanding number of persons engaging in B2C e-commerce. In 2019, some 1.48 billion persons, or close to one quarter of the world's population aged 15 and older, made purchases online (Table 2.5) ((UNCTAD, 2021[14])). This represented a 16.5% increase over the 1.27 billion e-consumers in 2017. While consumers bought mostly from domestic vendors, some 360 million made cross-border purchases, a 38.4% increase from 2017. As a result, the share of persons making cross-border purchases rose from 20% in 2017, to 25% in 2019.

Table 2.5. Number of online shoppers worldwide (in billion of persons), 2017-19

Type of purchase	2017	2018	2019
Cross-border	0.26	0.29	0.36
Domestic	1.01	1.09	1.12
Total	1.27	1.38	1.48

Source: UNCTAD, 2021.

In the OECD area, B2C e-commerce was more pronounced. Almost 60% of individuals bought products online in 2019, up from 38% in 2010 (OECD, 2020[11]). Within the area, the share of people buying online still varied significantly across countries, as well as across different product categories. Age, education, income and experience all influenced uptake. In Denmark, the Netherlands and the United Kingdom, more than 80% of adults shopped online, while in other countries, the participation level was 25%, or less. In 2018, the items most commonly purchased online were clothing, footwear and sporting goods, and travel products, followed by tickets for events, reading materials, movies and music, photographic, telecommunication and optical equipment, and food and grocery products. The trend towards online shopping is expected to continue, especially in light of the COVID-19 pandemic, with an ever-increasing number of persons buying products using mobile devices (OECD, 2020[11]). Existing evidence suggests that parcel trade during recent lockdowns largely involves ICT goods, medical products, appliances and leisure products such as games and toys (Sorescu, 2021[15]). In addition to purchasing items, consumers are also increasingly selling goods and services online. In 2019, nearly 20% of individuals in the European Union sold goods or services online, which was more than double the 2008 level.

With respect to trends, subscription services provided through e-commerce channels are becoming more popular (OECD, 2020[11]). Such subscriptions are characterized by regular and recurring payments for the repeated provision of a good or service. In the e-commerce context, this can include subscription to streaming digital products, such as movies, as well as subscriptions to products, such as food or cosmetics which deplete with use and require replenishment. Online technologies enable easy ordering of the goods and services, removing associated transaction costs and thus improving convenience for consumers. Firms, on the other hand, benefit from regular and ongoing revenue streams. Interestingly, connected devices that use streams of data through sensors, software and network connections have become linked with physical goods to make continuous or recurring purchases.

Risks of counterfeits offered on-line

The rapid advancements of e-commerce have enhanced consumer choice, and offered businesses new, flexible ways of market access. In fact the existing firm-level evidence shows that digital technologies enable firms (including SMEs), to become exporters (Andrenelli, 2019[16]). At the same time, there were concerns over the potential abuse of e-commerce to facilitate illicit trade in counterfeit goods. Indeed, there is ample evidence that the on-line environment has also attracted bad actors, who have found appealing the ease and low cost of offering not only of counterfeit products, but of all sorts of illicit goods ranging from fake pharmaceuticals and counterfeits to guns and narcotics.

In the context of counterfeit goods, concerns related to abuse of e-commerce, reflect the ease with which criminals can pollute with fakes e-commerce distribution channels. As mentioned above, it is relatively easy to set up e-commerce websites in most jurisdictions, as the large number (12 to 24 million) attests. Fraudsters who are intent on swindling consumers are thus in good position to establish a web presence, through which their fraudulent acts can be committed. Many of the fraudsters who establish sites are active traders of counterfeit and pirated products.

Consequently, the online environment offers great conditions for offering of many types of counterfeits, ranging from goods that pretend to be genuine and can be found on reputed online marketplaces, to poor quality goods, openly marketed as fakes. Put it differently, there are many types of so-called primary and secondary markets for counterfeits that can found online (Box 2.2). In primary markets, described for example in (OECD/EUIPO, 2016[1]) consumers are deceived, and purchase fake good believing they were genuine. These correspond for example to fraudulent sites that deceive consumers selling fake goods for genuine, or deceitful offerings at on-line platforms that mislead consumers and present counterfeit goods as if they were genuine. Secondary markets correspond to on-line offerings, in which consumers gets enough signals that a given good is counterfeit. This includes for example ill- described offers of apparently branded products at a very low price, goods openly described as fakes or offers of goods that are of seemingly good quality, but are still described as non-genuine (for example as "replicas").

Box 2.2. Consumer deception vs. knowing demand for fakes

The notion of *primary* and *secondary markets* refers to the two market segments targeted by counterfeiters. In primary markets, consumers are deceived and prices of counterfeit goods are expected to be close to those of legitimate products. In secondary markets, consumers knowingly purchase counterfeit goods, and larger price dispersions between genuine and fake are observed. Consumers that knowingly purchase an IP-infringing product may expect to pay a lower price for it than for a genuine product.

The quantitative analysis points that for products that are intensely targeted by counterfeiters (and hence for which large data samples are available), such as footwear, clothing, and leather goods secondary markets might be large. The presence of secondary market is much smaller in sectors, where consumption of counterfeits might cause significant health and safety risk, such as food or pharmaceuticals.

The distinction between primary and secondary markets described is critical to analyse the damages caused by counterfeiting. Every sale of a fake item on a primary market clearly represents a direct loss for industries. In secondary markets, however, only a share of consumers would have deliberately substituted their purchases of counterfeit products for legitimate ones. This is because in secondary markets consumers know what they are buying is fake and they decide to proceed with the purchase for a number of possible reasons.

As discussed below, the largest marketplace platform providers have developed mechanisms to undermine the bad actors who, knowingly or unknowingly, seek to sell counterfeit goods via e-commerce. Governments have also taken measures in this regard, but the challenges are great and remain of keen concern to all stakeholders, with some governments now actively pursuing legislation to address problems. Once detected, governments can act to have rogue websites taken down; the ease of re-establishing such websites using new domain names, however, is problematic.

In addition to national actions, a number of initiatives have been taken at the international level to combat the online sale of counterfeit items. INTERPOL, for example, has coordinated campaigns against the online sale of illicit drugs and medical devices (OECD/EUIPO, 2020[8]). Operation Pangea has been carried out since 2008, with the number of countries participating rising from 8, to a record 123 in 2017. Participating agencies carried out coordinated operational activities against illegal websites during the same week with a view towards identifying the criminal networks behind the trafficking (Table 2.6). During Pangea XI, which was carried out in 2018, police, customs and health regulatory authorities from 116 countries targeted the illicit online sale of medicines and medical products, resulting in 859 arrests worldwide and the seizure of USD 14 million worth of potentially dangerous pharmaceuticals. Almost one million packages were inspected during the week of action, with 500 tonnes of illicit pharmaceuticals seized worldwide. Seizures included anti-inflammatory medication, painkillers, erectile dysfunction pills, hypnotic and sedative agents, anabolic steroids, slimming pills and medicines for treating HIV, Parkinson's and diabetes. More than 110,000 medical devices including syringes, contact lenses, hearing aids and surgical instruments were also seized.

Table 2.6. Operation Pangea 2008-2018

Year (Pangea number)	Number of countries	Seizures		Number of arrests	Number of websites closed
		Quantity	Value (millions of USD)		
2008 (I)	10	NA	NA	NA	NA
2009 (II)	24	167,000 items	NA	22*	72
2010 (III)	45	1 million	2.6	NA	290
2011 (IV)	81	2.4 million items	6.3	55*	13,500
2012 (V)	100	3.75 million items	10.5	80	18,000
2013 (VI)	100	9.8 million items	41	58	9,000
2014 (VII)	111	9.4 million items	31	237	10,600
2015 (VIII)	115	20.7 million items	81	156	2,414
2016 (IX)	103	12.2 million items	53	393	4,932
2017 (X)	123	25 million items	51	400	3,584
2018 (XI)	116	500 tonnes	14	859	3,671

Note: * Arrested or under investigation.
NA: Not available.
Source: INTERPOL news releases at www.interpol.int/News-and-EventsOne of the main trends identified during the decade of Pangea operations is the continuous growth of unauthorised and unregulated online pharmacies, which are capitalising on increasing consumer demand worldwide.[6] Also of note, criminals are shipping packages containing smaller numbers of pills and tablets to avoid the more stringent checks which have become routine in many countries.[7]

The speed at which e-commerce expands, and the forms it takes, are being influenced by technological developments and the policy environments governing e-commerce transactions. Much attention is being paid at national and international levels to ensure that markets are competitive, transparent and fair. Importantly, some of this issues refer to abuse of on-line environment in counterfeiting, as they affect, directly or indirectly, the online environment, in which the bad actors, and consumers operate. Some of the key challenges and opportunities affecting markets are discussed below.

Consumer protection

E-commerce will thrive to the extent that manufacturers, sellers and consumers are able to establish and strengthen trust. Consumers, for example, face challenges related to online information disclosure, misleading and unfair commercial practices, confirmation and payment, fraud and identity theft, product safety, and dispute resolution and redress (OECD, 2020[11]).

Certain "dark patterns" have been observed that can undermine consumer interests and weaken trust. These include tactics employed by businesses in websites and apps to steer or deceive consumers into making unintended or potentially harmful decisions (OECD, 2020[11]). Some of these tactics can be also used on sites offering counterfeit goods. Examples include using opt-out check boxes to sneak unwanted items into online shopping carts, and enticing consumers into subscriptions that are easy to start but difficult to cancel. Another challenge concerns the reliability of product evaluations and reviews. An OECD survey on consumer trust in peer-platform marketplaces revealed that 73% of consumers identified the ability to see ratings and reviews as an important trust mechanism; it may be difficult, however, for consumers to distinguish legitimate reviews and evaluations from contrived or fake reviews and evaluations.

Consumers have also been affected by targeted online advertising, which can affect consumer interests in various ways. Developments in AI and machine learning, coupled with online data collection, have enabled cost-effective, targeted advertising on an unprecedented scale (OECD, 2020[11]). Such advertising uses information such as age, gender, location, education level, interests, online shopping behaviour and search history. Complementary technologies track user interaction with online ads to determine the effectiveness of advertising campaigns. They also provide the infrastructure for advertising payments to be tied to specific user outcomes such as "clicks", webpage visits or purchases. These developments can provide both benefits and risks for consumers. Benefits include more targeted, relevant and timely ads. These could reduce search costs and improve awareness of relevant products and identification of, and access to, better deals. Online advertising also funds a range of nominally free online services, including search services, social networking services and digital news outlets. Risks include longstanding concerns around advertising's potential to mislead or deceive, as well as new concerns. Emerging issues include: i) consumers' inability to identify some forms of online advertising, ii) the impacts on consumer trust online, iii) the enhanced ability for online advertising to prey on consumer biases and vulnerabilities, iv) the increased threats from "malvertising"[8] and v) the risks associated with increased collection and sharing of personal data.

Governments have played a role in addressing concerns, with a view towards protecting consumers from certain harmful practices. One area which has received considerable attention is the use of default settings in an e-commerce setting (OECD, 2020[11]). Behavioural studies suggest that consumers will generally accept defaults, in the form of pre-checked boxes, even though doing so may be contrary to their interest. In negative option marketing, for example, a customer's failure to take affirmative action to reject or cancel an agreement is taken as consent. Consumers can thus unwittingly opt in for additional goods or services with associated fees or charges. Moreover, pre-checked boxes or other default settings can result in consumers i) automatically signing up for additional goods or services, ii) unwittingly making financial commitments, or iii) disclosing personal data or marketing material that they might otherwise prefer not to share. In the case of the European Union pre-ticked boxes online have been banned under its Consumer Rights Directive. Similarly, UK consumers are not bound by charges for any goods that are sold by way of pre-ticked boxes (Box 2.3). In the United States, under the 2010 Restore Online Shoppers' Confidence Act, businesses must obtain a consumer's express consent before charging for any goods or services purchased online. In addition, for online goods or services sold through a negative option feature, businesses must also provide consumers with details of the transaction and a simple means to opt-out of any reoccurring charges.

> **Box 2.3. EU Consumer Rights Directive**
>
> The EU *Consumer Rights Directive*, which came into effect on 13 June 2014, is designed to strengthen consumer rights by giving consumers the same rights across the European Union, while striking an appropriate right balance between consumer protection and business competitiveness. A number of provisions concern online transactions.
>
> - No more cost-traps on the Internet. Online shoppers need to confirm that they accept paying for something before they are charged. What is included in the price needs to be clearly indicated.
> - No more pre-ticked boxes. Pre-ticked boxes on websites involving additional payments (such as priority boarding for airline reservations are banned.
> - Online shoppers will not have to pay for any charges of which they are not clearly informed before they make a purchase.
> - The period for consumers to pull out of any distance purchase (e.g. something bought online) is extended from a minimum of 7 days, to a uniform 14 days across the European Union; the cancellation can be for any reason. When a seller hasn't clearly informed the consumer about the right to cancel the purchases, the return period is extended to a year.
> - Consumers will be allowed to pull out from online auction purchases from professional sellers.
> - Traders must refund consumers within 14 days of cancellation, including standard delivery costs. Regarding goods, the trader can postpone the reimbursement until the goods are returned by the consumer or the consumer provides evidence that these goods have been sent to the trader.
> - Consumers will be given a standard EU form to use if they want to cancel their purchases. This will make it easier for them to get out of contracts concluded outside of their home country.
> - Traders wanting consumers to pay for the return of goods after cancellation must clearly inform them beforehand, and give at least an estimate of the cost for returning bulky goods.
>
> Source: See https://ec.europa.eu/info/sites/default/files/crd_arc_factsheet-consumer_en.pdf.

At the OECD level, the challenges facing consumers were addressed by countries in 2016, through the adoption of a *Recommendation of the Council on Consumer Protection in E-commerce*, which seeks to safeguard consumers who purchase goods and services online. The recommendation provides specific guidance to governments and other stakeholders aimed at (OECD, 2016b[17]):

- Providing transparent and effective protection that is not less than the level of protection afforded in other forms of commerce.
- Establishing fair business, advertising and marketing practices.
- Ensuring that online disclosures are clear and accurate.
- Ensuring that confirmation processes that are clear and unambiguous.
- Establishing payment mechanisms that are easy to use, secure and provide adequate protection.
- Providing dispute resolution and redress mechanisms that are fair, easy-to-use, transparent and effective.
- Safeguarding the privacy and security of consumers.
- Promoting consumer education, awareness and digital competence.

The guidelines provide a blueprint for governments and business for addressing key concerns; successful implementation would help build the trust that is needed to expand e-commerce in the future.

Social media

Businesses have become active on social media platforms,[9] which are being used by businesses to deepen interactions with consumers. The pervasiveness of social networks, which are the most popular online activity in most countries, were used by nearly three-quarters of Internet users in the OECD in 2019 (OECD, 2020[11]). Businesses have taken note; more than half in the OECD had a social media presence in 2017, up from one-third in 2013. As in other areas, there is a marked contrast between countries. Usage ranges ranged from over 65% in Iceland, Norway, Brazil, the Netherlands, Ireland and Denmark, to below 30% in Japan, Poland and Mexico. Medium and large enterprises are the predominant users. In 2017, fewer than one in three small firms in the OECD used social media compared to almost three-quarters of large firms. Growth in e-commerce, combined with similar growth in social media usage has encouraged companies to turn to influencer marketing[10] and user generated content to promote brand awareness (Phaneuf, 2021[18]).

Businesses primarily use social media for developing the enterprise's image and marketing products, as well as to obtain or respond to customer opinions, reviews or questions (OECD, 2020[11]). They may also use social media to involve customers in the development or innovation of goods or services. The use of social media for commercial purposes (referred to as "social commerce") is booming, with US retail social commerce sales forecast to rise by 34.8% in 2021, to $36.1 billion, representing 4.3% of all retail e-commerce sales (Phaneuf, 2021[18]). While fashion categories including apparel and accessories are the largest segment of social commerce, electronics and home decor are also significant. Companies can use influencers, consumer call to actions, and user generated content, to capitalize on the power of social commerce.

Social media are attractive for counterfeiters for a number of reasons. The potential number of users available on social media is immense. For example Facebook alone has well over 2.5 billion users. In addition, recent research suggest that, consumers are already very receptive to the idea of purchasing items from social media.[11] Furthermore, social media offer many marketing tools that can be applied to segment audience by gender, location, age etc. Last, social media platforms offer many additional privacy options abused by criminals groups offering counterfeiters, such as closed groups or ephemeral content, which poses additional challenges for law enforcement authorities.

Recently, social media have been frequently abused to distribute counterfeit goods, to support IP infringement through other channels and to provide information on such activities (EUIPO, 2021[19]). Counterfeiters have adapted their tactics depending on the type of site, and learned how to market fakes on these sites in a professional manner, and the abuse of social media platforms by counterfeiters has been confirmed by systemic, empirical studies. For example (EUIPO, 2021[20]) focused on key social media platforms in the EU and identified conversations related to the categories and brands chosen to represent physical products. It found that 11% of these conversation could be possibly related to counterfeits. This finding highlights that that social media platforms are tools for recurrent IPR infringement for both physical products and digital content.

Privacy and data protection

In order to engage in e-commerce, consumers are in many instances required to provide potentially sensitive personal and financial information, the unauthorized sharing or leaking of which could cause serious problems for the individuals concerned. Indeed, public perception studies in the last few years suggest that individuals are increasingly concerned about the use and protection of their personal data

(OECD, 2020[11]). Reflecting growing concerns, national governments worldwide are strengthening their data protection frameworks and policies.

One of the most prominent examples is the EU's General Data Protection Regulation (GDPR) that frames data protection and privacy in the European Union and the European Economic Area (Box 2.4). Following the 2016-adopted regulation, collection and use of personal data of customers located in the EU must be carried out with their full consent. In addition, personal data must be stored securely, and be made available at their request. It has had a clear impact on e-commerce activities, and some studies suggest it reduced to some extent the volume of e-commerce activities in the EU (Goldberg, 2019[21]).

Box 2.4. EU General Data Protection Regulation (GDPR)

The EU *General Data Protection Regulation,* which was adopted on 14 April 2016 has two general aims: to augment and clarify peoples' control over the collection, use and storage of their personal data and to streamline the related regulatory frameworks.

The GDPR is a regulation, and it is directly binding in the EEA countries (EU countries plus Iceland, Liechtenstein and Norway). It became enforceable on 25 May 2018.

The GDPR provides regulations to entities that collect, store and process personal data of people located in the EEA. Importantly, GDPR applies to any enterprise — not only those located in the EEA – that process personal information of people inside the EEA.

The GDPR frames a number of specific aspects, including, rights of the data subject, duties of data controllers or processors, potential transfers of personal data to third countries, supervisory authorities, cooperation among member states, remedies, liability or penalties for breach of rights, etc.

Following the introduction of GDPR, many economies have also introduced similar provision, being inspired by the EU Regulation. It included some OECD Countries as Chile, Japan, Korea and Turkey.

Sources: See https://gdpr-info.eu/ and https://ec.europa.eu/info/sites/default/files/data-protection-factsheet-sme-obligations_en.pdf.

Of note is also the California Consumer Privacy Act (CCPA), which came into force on 1 January 2020. It creates new consumer rights for the collection, processing, retention and sharing of personal data, and represents a fundamental re-thinking of privacy rights in the United States, which does not have comprehensive or overarching federal privacy law (OECD, 2020[11]). Businesses subject to the CCPA are obliged to provide notice to consumers at or before data collection, respond to consumer requests, disclose financial incentives offered in exchange for personal information and maintain detailed records.

Phishing and pharming

Phishing, the practice whereby attackers disguise themselves as a trustworthy entity with a view towards tricking parties into providing sensitive personal information, is a growing problem that, if unchecked could significantly affect the willingness of consumers to engage in some types of e-commerce. Phishing messages often include links to malicious sites that are increasingly difficult for end-users to detect without using some type of automated protection (OECD, 2020[11]). Broad untargeted phishing campaigns aim to collect information by directing users to fake e-commerce or financial websites. More sophisticated emails target specific individuals to plant malware in an organization's information system (spear-phishing).

Pharming is a risk related to phishing. It is an offensive action carried out by criminals to redirect on-line traffic from a legitimate website to another site, usually offering illicit goods or content, including counterfeit goods.

In the European Union, surveys indicate that an average of 30% of EU Internet users were victims of phishing in 2019, while about 15% were victims of pharming (OECD, 2020[11]).[12] Norway, also included in the survey, registered the highest levels of both phishing (60%) and pharming (30%). In some countries, the levels were less than 15%. Various factors might contribute to explain the differences, including lack of awareness/understanding of phishing attempts and/or the inability to identify them.

Payment mechanisms

Payment mechanisms used in e-commerce are characterized by a high degree of protection, thereby providing the consumers with the security that they need to engage in transactions with sellers with whom they may have little experience. The protection is offered on a competitive basis by charge card providers, with the level of protection varying by card type. Credit cards, for example, generally provide a far higher level of protection than debit cards. Additional protection provided by platform operators serve to further boost consumer confidence, helping to create a low-risk trading environment which focuses on maximizing consumer satisfaction.

The means of payment have expanded in recent years, providing consumers with considerable choice in how they can pay for their purchases. The relatively new forms of payment include digital wallets, mobile money and cryptocurrencies (OECD, 2020[11]). *Digital wallets* act as an intermediary that manages payment information on both sides of a transaction, without disclosing the payment details to either party. Some wallets, like PayPal, directly process payments, transferring money between buyers and sellers; others, like Google Wallet, transfer financial details between the payment processors of the parties involved in a transaction. Mobile wallets are a sub-type of digital wallets, with mobile-specific features and services which can be used to make purchases online. However, they are also increasingly used in point-of-sale transactions, by, for example, street vendors and brick-and-mortar stores, using connected devices.

Mobile payments, or *mobile money* are payments that are made using via mobile communication networks; they do not necessarily require that a party have a relationship with a financial services provider and are therefore particularly useful for persons who do not have bank accounts (OECD, 2020[11]). The mobile money is mediated by mobile network operators, who use a system of agents to accept cash from persons. The value of the cash is then stored in a digital wallet, which can then be used for digital payments to others. Mobile money is typically associated with a mobile phone number and often uses two-factor authentication through a personal identification number issued at the point of registration.

Distributed ledger technologies, also known as *cryptocurrencies* (like bitcoin), operate through a distributed database which is independent from traditional financial institutions (OECD, 2020[11]). They provide a means for making anonymous, validated transfers of financial value. Online companies accepting Bitcoin as payment include a number of multi-billion-dollar firms, such as NewEgg (which is a consumer electronics firm), Overstock (which primarily sells furniture) and Shopify (which is a major e-commerce platform). Moreover, extensions of blockchain-enabled payments may hold more potential for e-commerce. These include use of "smart contracts", which are self-executing and deterministic software protocols that only transfer value after particular conditions are met. Such contracts could hold particular promise for e-commerce when combined with connected devices. For example, a blockchain-enabled, connected washing machine could initiate an e-commerce transaction through a smart contract when it detects that it is out of detergent. Blockchain technology could therefore enable e-commerce transactions between connected devices rather than simply between individuals and firms.

Suppliers of counterfeits online are benefiting from the move away from a cash economy, and actively leverage potential payment options. Online sales of counterfeits are illicit operations that require accessible and reliable payment processing to transfer money from customer to merchant. Brand owners and payment system providers have been engaging in a number of co-operative efforts, and some successes in this area have been reported. Restricting the ability for criminals to receive payment for their online sales through mainstream online payment system deters potential consumers, and reduces the profitability of the business. However, brand owner highlight that improvement is needed, including development of clear policies. (INTA, 2020[22])

On the other hand counterfeiters adapt their tactics to respond to these actions. For example, as report in a study by (Tian, 2018[23]), online counterfeit luxury goods merchants use criminal payment facilitators, called *bullet-proof credit card processors*, that are offering online credit card processing services that are tailored to accept payments for counterfeits purchased online. The *bullet-proof processors* rely on established shell companies that appear to sell online regular goods. These sites are not functional and do not accept payments; they are used only to facilitate payments made for counterfeits through the processors.

Small Parcels

E-commerce has given certain distribution channels a big boost, providing a means for businesses to bypass retail outlets and ship small quantities of items directly to individual consumers in a cost-effective manner. The success of this business strategy is borne out by the profitability and growth of the largest e-commerce market platforms. The distribution channels that have been most favourably affected are the post and local and international delivery services such as Fedex, UPS and DHL. In the case of the post, traffic in domestic and international letters has declined sharply over time, falling by close to one third from 2001 to 2019 (Table 2.7). On the other hand, fuelled by e-commerce, the volume of parcel traffic, both domestic and international more than quadrupled during the same time period, rising to 21.3 billion items in 2019.[13] In the five-year period 2015-2019 alone, parcel traffic rose by more than 70%.

Table 2.7. Processing of letters and parcels by postal authorities in recent years

Year	Letters			Parcels		
	Domestic	International	Total	Domestic	International	Total
		Billions			Millions	Billions
2001	416	6.9	423	4.8	43	4.8
2010	356	4.3	360	8	62	8.1
2015	310	3.3	313	12.2	115	12.3
2016	301	3.1	304	14.6	133	14.7
2017	303	2.9	306	16.3	174	16.5
2018	290	2.7	293	18.4	179	18.6
2019	284	2.6	287	21.1	192	21.3

Source: UPU (see https://www.upu.int/en/Universal-Postal-Union/Activities/Research-Publications/Postal-Statistics#query-the-database, accessed 18 July 2021.

While data are not yet available for 2020 and 2021, the impact of COVID-19 could well have accelerated growth in parcel trade. In the United States, for example, mail volumes declined precipitously in FY2020[14] as marketers restrained from spending and adapted to changes in consumer behaviour (USPS, 2020/21[24]). Package volumes, on the other hand, rose by 19% from FY2019 to FY2020, to 7.3 billion pieces as people minimized in-person shopping and ordered goods delivered to their homes.

Postal services are keen on strengthening their participation in e-commerce. The USPS, for example, has focused on growing e-commerce and implementing marketing campaigns to increase business by offering day-specific delivery, improved tracking, text alerts and up to USD 100 of free insurance included on most

Priority Mail packages. At the international level, the UPU updated its e-commerce guide (originally published in 2014), in 2020, to include new and expanded information on recent trends, business models, e-commerce key elements, strategies and UPU enablers to facilitate e-commerce (UPU, 2020[25]).

As noted, the ability of suppliers to furnish consumers with goods in a cost-effective manner via the post and related delivery services has been highly beneficial for the parties concerned. It has, however, provided an opening for those involved in illicit trade to carry out their operations with little risk of detection as the quantities of merchandise shipped in individual parcels and letter packets tend to be small and the shipments are intermingled with billions of legitimately traded items. The problem is a significant one that commands considerable attention from enforcement authorities.[15] Trade in counterfeits via parcels is an important vehicle for facilitating the illicit trade, which is reflected in seizures by border officials. In 2019, some 77% of seizures involved items shipped by post or courier services (OECD/EUIPO, 2021[4]). Most of the seizures involved a small number of items, with mail accounting for only 12.1% of the total number of items seized.[16] The challenges in combatting the counterfeits are ongoing as the criminal networks involved are constantly adapting their techniques to evade the efforts of enforcement authorities to intercept the illicit products (OECD/EUIPO, 2020[8]).

COVID-19

The COVID-19 crisis turns the attention to the online environment. Law enforcement officials have reported a huge shift to cybercrime (fraud, phishing, etc.) while criminals take advantage of people working at home with less secure infrastructure. According to law enforcement authorities, in the EU e-commerce is a predominant medium to send fraudulent COVID-19 related products. Under the confinement, consumers also turn to online markets to fulfil their needs. This has sparked a marked uptick in cyber-related offenses.

For example, since March 2020, at least 100 000 new domain names containing COVID-19 related words (e.g., Covid, corona or virus) were registered to sell related medical items. The Dark Net is also playing a role in the rapid spread of falsified medicines, as COVID-19 is part of the Dark Net's keywords.

In the US, the challenge is to ensure a safe and lawful e-commerce for businesses, consumers and intellectual rights holders. Following the e-commerce boom, the huge number of small packages, with a declared value of under USD 800, poses data constraints since only minimal data are required when sending them. In this context, relevant data are essential to identify bad actors and oblige them to free up the trade line through the debarment and suspension process (which makes the bad actors list publicly known). In this framework, the Anti-Counterfeiting Consortium to Identify Online Nefarious Actors (ACTION) Plan was created.

Online platforms tend to be aware of these risks. For example, during the pandemic, Amazon detected price gouging and ill-described (including counterfeit) goods. Amazon reacted quickly and has worked closely with legal and communication teams, and collaborated with EU law enforcement to share information related to fraudulent goods related to COVID-19 pandemics.

References

Amazon (2021), *Brand Protection Report*, https://assets.aboutamazon.com/96/a0/90f229d54c8cba5072b2c4e021f7/amz-brand-report.pdf. [41]

Andrenelli, A. (2019), "Electronic transmissions and international trade - shedding new light on the moratorium debate", *OECD Trade Policy Papers*, Vol. 233, https://doi.org/10.1787/57b50a4b-en. [16]

DHS (2020), *Combating Trafficking in Counterfeit and Pirated Goods*, US Department of Homeland Security, Washington, https://www.dhs.gov/sites/default/files/publications/20_0124_plcy_counterfeit-pirated-goods-report_01.pdf. [32]

eBay (2021), *2020 Global Transparency Report*, http://www.ebaymainstreet.com/sites/default/files/2021-05/2020-eBay-Global-Transparency-Report.pdf. [40]

EC (2017), *Overview of the functioning of the Memorandum of Understanding on the sale of counterfeit goods via the internet, SWD(2017) 430 final*, https://ec.europa.eu/docsroom/documents/26602. [30]

EC (2016), *Memorandum of Understanding: 21 June 2016, Ref. Ares(2016)3934515 26/07/2016*, European Commission, Brussels, https://ec.europa.eu/docsroom/documents/43321/attachments/2/translations/en/renditions/native. [29]

EC (2013), *Report from the Commission to the European Parliament and the Council on the Functioning of the Memorandum of Understanding on the Sale of Counterfeit Goods via the Internet, COM(2013), 209 final,*, European Commission, Brussels,, http://Ref. Ares(2016). [28]

EC (2020b), *Report on the functioning of the Memorandum of Understanding on the sale of Counterfeit Goods on the internet, SWD(2020) 166 final/2*, European Commission, Brussels, https://ec.europa.eu/docsroom/documents/42701. [27]

EUIPO (2021), *Monitoring and analysing social media in relation to IPR infringement Report*, https://euipo.europa.eu/tunnel-web/secure/webdav/guest/document_library/observatory/documents/reports/2021_Monitoring_and_analysing_social_media_in_relation_to_IPR_Infringement_Report/2021_Monitoring_and_analysing_social_media_in_relation_to_IPR_Infringem. [20]

EUIPO (2021), *New and existing trends in using social media for IP infringement activities and good practices to address them*, https://euipo.europa.eu/tunnel-web/secure/webdav/guest/document_library/observatory/documents/reports/2021_Social_Media/2021_Social_Media_Discussion_Paper_FullR_en.pdf. [19]

GCIG (2016), *One Internet, Centre for International Governance Innovation and Chatham House*, http://www.cigionline.org/documents/1045/gcig_final_report_-_with_cover.pdf. [39]

Goldberg, S. (2019), "Regulating Privacy Online: An Economic Evaluation of the GDPR", *SSRN Working Paper*, http://dx.doi.org/10.2139/ssrn.3421731. [21]

Group, I. (2020), *IP Crime and Enforcement Report*, IP Crime Group Secretariat, Concept House, Newport, https://assets.publishing.service.gov.uk/government/uploads/system/uploads/attachment_data/file/913644/ip-crime-report-2019-20.pdf. [31]

INTA (2020), *Addressing the Sale of Counterfeits on the Internet*, https://www.inta.org/wp-content/uploads/public-files/advocacy/committee-reports/Addressing_the_Sale_of_Counterfeits_on_the_Internet_June_2021_edit.pdf. [22]

OCDE/EUIPO (2021), *Misuse of Containerized Maritime Shipping in the Global Trade of Counterfeits*, Éditions OCDE, Paris,, https://doi.org/10.1787/e39d8939-en. [9]

OECD (2021), *COVID-19 vaccine and the Threat of Illicit Trade, Chair's Summary Note*, https://www.oecd.org/gov/illicit-trade/summary-note-covid-19-vaccine-and-the-threat-of-illicit-trade.pdf. [35]

OECD (2021), *Illicit trade: Discussions with stakeholders*, unpublished. [26]

OECD (2020), *Illicit Trade in a Time of Crisis. Chair's Summary Note*, https://www.oecd.org/gov/illicit-trade/oecd-webinar-illicit-trade-time-crisis-23-april.pdf. [10]

OECD (2020), *OECD Digital Economy Outlook 2020*, OECD Publishing, Paris, https://doi.org/10.1787/bb167041-en. [11]

OECD (2020), *Trade in Fake Medicines at the Time of the Covid-19 Pandemics. Chair's Summary Note*, https://www.oecd.org/gov/illicit-trade/oecd-fake-medicines-webinar-june-10-summary-note.pdf. [34]

OECD (2018), *Governance Frameworks to Counter Illicit Trade*, OECD Publishing, Paris,, https://doi.org/10.1787/9789264291652-en. [33]

OECD (2011), *OECD Council Recommendation on Principles for Internet Policy Making*, OECD, Paris, https://www.oecd.org/sti/ieconomy/49258588.pdf. [37]

OECD (2008), *The Economic Impact of Counterfeiting and Piracy*, Éditions OCDE, Paris, https://doi.org/10.1787/9789264045521-en. [13]

OECD (2016a), *Ministerial Declaration on the Digital Economy*, OECD, http://www.oecd.org/digital/Digital-Economy-Ministerial-Declaration-2016.pdf. [38]

OECD (2016b), *Recommendation of the Council on Consumer Protection in E-commerce*, OECD, Paris, https://legalinstruments.oecd.org/en/instruments/OECD-LEGAL-0422. [17]

OECD/EUIPO (2021), *Global Trade in Fakes: a Worrying Threat*, OECD Publishing, https://www.oecd.org/publications/global-trade-in-fakes-74c81154-en.htm. [4]

OECD/EUIPO (2020), *Trade in Counterfeit Pharmaceutical Products*, Illicit Trade, OECD Publishing, Paris, https://dx.doi.org/10.1787/a7c7e054-en. [8]

OECD/EUIPO (2019), *Trends in Trade in Counterfeit and Pirated Goods*, OECD Publishing, Paris,, https://doi.org/10.1787/g2g9f533-en. [3]

OECD/EUIPO (2018), *Misuse of Small Parcels for Trade in Counterfeit Goods: Facts and Trends*, OECD Publishing, Paris, https://doi.org/10.1787/9789264307858-en. [7]

OECD/EUIPO (2018), *Trade in Counterfeit Goods and Free Trade Zones: Evidence from Recent Trends*, OECD Publishing, Paris/EUIPO, Alicante, https://doi.org/10.1787/9789264289550-en. [5]

OECD/EUIPO (2018), *Why Do Countries Export Fakes?: The Role of Governance Frameworks, Enforcement and Socio-economic Factors*, OECD Publishing, Paris/EUIPO, Alicante, https://doi.org/10.1787/9789264302464-en. [6]

OECD/EUIPO (2017), *Mapping the Real Routes of Trade in Fake Goods, Illicit Trade*, OECD Publishing, Paris, https://doi.org/10.1787/9789264278349-en. [2]

OECD/EUIPO (2016), *Trade in Counterfeit and Pirated Goods: Mapping the Economic Impact, Illicit Trade*, OECD Publishing, Paris, https://doi.org/10.1787/9789264252653-en. [1]

Phaneuf, A. (2021), *Social Commerce 2021: Social media and Ecommerce Convergence Trends Brings Growth Opportunity for Brands, Insider Inc.,*, http://www.businessinsider.com/social-commerce-brand-trends-marketing-strategies. [18]

S. Goldberg, G. (2019), "Regulating Privacy Online: An Economic Evaluation of the GDPR", *SSRN Working Paper*, http://dx.doi.org/10.2139/ssrn.3421731. [42]

Sorescu, S. (2021), "Trade in the time of parcels", *OECD Trade Policy Papers*, Vol. 249, https://doi.org/10.1787/0faac348-en. [15]

Tian, H. (2018), *Bullet-proof payment processors*, https://ieeexplore.ieee.org/document/8376208. [23]

UNCTAD (2021), *Estimates of global e-commerce 2019 and preliminary assessment of COVID-19 impact on online retail 2020*, United Nations Conference on Trade and Development, Geneva, https://unctad.org/system/files/official-document/tn_unctad_ict4d18_en.pdf. [14]

UNICRI (2020), *"Cyber-crime during the COVID-19 Pandemic"*, http://www.unicri.it/news/cyber-crime-during-covid-19-pandemic. [12]

UPU (2020), *E-commerce Guide*, Universal Postal Union, Berne, https://www.upu.int/UPU/media/upu/publications/Final-November-update-UPU-E-Commerce-Guide_2020_EN.pdf. [25]

USPS (2020/21), *FY 2020 Annual Report to Congress*, United States Postal Service, https://about.usps.com/what/financials/annual-reports/fy2020.pdf. [24]

WCO (2020), *Illicit Trade Report 2019*, WCO, Brussels,, http://www.wcoomd.org/-/media/wco/public/global/pdf/topics/enforcement-and-compliance/activities-and-programmes/illicit-trade-report/itr_2019_en.pdf?db=web. [36]

Notes

¹ The OECD defines e-commerce transactions as those involving the sale or purchase of goods or services, conducted over computer networks by methods specifically designed for the purpose of receiving or placing of orders. The goods or services are ordered by those methods, but the payment and the ultimate delivery of the goods or services do not have to be conducted online. An e-commerce transaction can be between enterprises, households, individuals, governments, and other public or private organisations. To be included are orders made over the web, extranet or electronic data interchange. The type is defined by the method of placing the order. To be excluded are orders made by telephone calls, facsimile or manually typed e-mail. See https://stats.oecd.org/glossary/detail.asp?ID=4721

² Other segments include consumer to business (C2B), consumer to government and (C2G) and business to government (B2G).

³ See www.census.gov/retail/index.html.

⁴ See www.ons.gov.uk/businessindustryandtrade/retailindustry/timeseries/j4mc/drsi .

⁵ See https://wpforms.com/ecommerce-statistics/.

⁶ See www.europol.europa.eu/newsroom/news/millions-of-medicines-seized-in-largest-operation-against-illicit-online-pharmacies.

⁷ See www.interpol.int/en/News-and-Events/News/2018/Illicit-online-pharmaceuticals-500-tonnes-seized-in-global-operation.

⁸ The use of advertising to spread malware.

⁹ Facebook, Instagram, Pinterest, TikTok and WeChat are examples of social media platforms.

¹⁰ Influencers are people who have the ability to influence others' beliefs, opinions or in the case of e-commerce, purchasing decisions.

¹¹ See https://www.redpoints.com/blog/the-growth-of-fake-products-on-social-media/.

¹² Pharming involves an Internet user being redirected to fake websites that ask for personal information.

¹³ The data on parcels does not include the considerable number of items that are sent in letter packets, data on which are not readily available.

¹⁴ The year ending on 30 September 2020.

¹⁵ See https://www.oecd.org/newsroom/trade-in-fake-goods-is-now-33-of-world-trade-and-rising.htm.

¹⁶ The number of seaborne seizures was far lower, but the number of items seized was considerably higher as the counterfeits tend to be shipped in bulk.

3 The trade in fakes: A first glance

This chapter presents the results of a quantitative exercise to study the relations between e-commerce and trade in counterfeit goods.

The qualitative evidence outlined in the previous chapter suggests that e-commerce provides an increasingly attractive means to facilitate the trade in counterfeit goods for a large range of product categories. The purpose of this analysis is to discern if there is a positive correlation between measures of e-commerce and trade in counterfeits. To accomplish this, three datasets from Eurostat, the World Bank, and the United Nations Conference on Trade and Development (UNCTAD) will be used to calculate correlations between e-commerce and the number and value of counterfeit customs seizures.

These correlations between e-commerce activity and illicit trade in fakes, become stronger for indicators of illicit trade in counterfeits misusing small parcels. This suggests that illicit goods purchased through on-line transactions are often shipped with small parcels, sent either by mail or express and postal services.

It is important to note that this section simply analyses correlations between e-commerce and counterfeit illicit trade. With that said, the information and correlations from this section justify that deeper analysis is necessary to further understand e-commerce's role in shaping global illicit trade.

Data

Following the approach taken in the previous studies, including the (OECD/EUIPO, 2016[1]), (OECD/EUIPO, 2019[3]) and (OECD/EUIPO, 2021[4]) reports, the analysis in this report is based on international trade statistics and customs seizures of infringing products. It also uses aggregated indicators on e-commerce.

Trade data

The trade statistics are based on the United Nations (UN) Comtrade database (based on the value of merchandise assigned by customs officials, i.e. the landed customs value). With 171 reporting economies and 247 partner economies, the database covers a majority of world trade and is considered the most comprehensive trade database available. Products are registered based on the six-digit Harmonised System (HS) (an international commodity classification system, developed and maintained by the World Customs Organization [WCO]), which means the level of detail in the data is high. Data used in this study are based on landed customs value. In most instances, this is the same as the transaction value appearing on accompanying invoices. Landed customs value includes the insurance and freight charges incurred when transporting goods from the economy of origin to the economy of importation.

Seizure data

Data on customs seizures originate from national customs administrations. This report relies on customs seizure data from the WCO, the European Commission's Directorate-General for Taxation and Customs

Union (DG TAXUD) and from the United States Department of Homeland Security (DHS). The latter submitted seizure data from US Customs and Border Protection (CBP), the American customs agency, and from the US Immigration and Customs Enforcement (ICE).

In each year analysed (2017, 2018 and 2019), the total number of customs seizures of counterfeit and pirated goods worldwide consistently exceeded 130 000. Overall, the unified database on customs seizures of IP-infringing goods includes almost 465 000 observations, as compared to the 428 000 recorded from 2011-13 (OECD/EUIPO, 2016[1]).

The database contains a wealth of information about illicit goods that can be used for quantitative and qualitative analysis. In most cases for each seizure the database reports: date of seizure, mode of transport of fake products, departure and destination economies, general statistical category of seized goods as well as their detailed description, name of legitimate brand owner, number of seized products and their approximate value. In addition, some customs data contains information related to e-commerce. In particular, some EU countries indicate in their data if the seized product was purchased on-line. The data contains a check-box, where customs officers indicate if it was the case.

A detailed analysis of the data reveals a set of limitations. Some of these limitations deal with discrepancies between the datasets, while others involve differing product classification levels or outliers in terms of seized goods or provenance economies. All limitations were thoroughly discussed in the (OECD/EUIPO, 2016[1]), (OECD/EUIPO, 2019[3]) and (OECD/EUIPO, 2021[4]) reports, and a methodological way forward was proposed for each limitation. This report also relies on the same methodology presented and discussed in the 2021 study, and it employs the same solutions to the seizure-data limitations.

E-commerce data

Measuring e-commerce is challenging since e-commerce definitions differ in various contexts, as discussed in the introductory section. Just like there is no single definition, there is no single measure that captures the scope of e-commerce within an economy. However, existing measures of aggregate components can still be used to uncover correlations related to e-commerce. These measures can be found in some datasets that approximate several dimensions of e-commerce, from consumer-related aspects to the enabling environment for e-commerce. These proxies will be used to calculate the correlation between e-commerce and illicit trade. These datasets come from:

- Eurostat,
- the World Bank, and
- the United Nations Conference on Trade and Development (UNCTAD)

Eurostat. For EU Member States, the 2019 Eurostat ICT Survey on Access and Usage can be used in analysis related to e-commerce, both domestic and cross-border. Two sections in the survey reveal the share of individuals who have purchased a good or service online during the prior three months, a finding that can be used as a proxy for e-commerce within an economy. This variable was combined with global customs seizures data from destination countries to draw a correlation. In addition, different specifications within the dataset enable a deeper comparison between the frequency and the value of global customs seizures as well as global customs seizures shipped by mail and express courier (EC).

World Bank. The World Bank Global Findex is a survey carried out every three years on how adults save, borrow, make payments and manage risk in 140 countries. In this data set, the variable "used the internet to buy something online in the past year" can be used a proxy of online purchase. The information provided by this variable is quite like Eurostat data but differs in two key areas. Firstly, the World Bank Index database in this report refers to 2017 data. Secondly, the World Bank database has a broader scope, as it is a worldwide survey rather than a regional one. Like in the Eurostat analysis, this proxy of e-commerce purchase was combined with customs seizures data by destination country to calculate correlations.

UNCTAD. The UNCTAD E-commerce Index measures the extent to which economies are prepared to support online shopping. The index relies on four non-weighted factors:

1. Account ownership at a financial institution or with a mobile-money-service provider (% of population ages 15+) from the World Bank Findex database
2. Individuals using the Internet (% of population) from the International Telecommunication Union (ITU)
3. Postal Reliability Index from the Universal Postal Union (UPU)
4. Secure Internet servers (per 1 million people) from the World Bank

To draw correlations between e-commerce and illicit trade, the 2019 UNCTAD E-commerce index was combined with the global customs seizures by destination country.

The regression analysis will be divided into two subsections. One section will look at correlations between e-commerce and overall illicit trade flows. The second section will examine e-commerce's correlation with illicit trade transported through small parcels. Since e-commerce has significantly contributed to the rise of small parcel shipping, it can be expected that the e-commerce's correlation with small parcel illicit trade will be more significant than its correlation with overall counterfeit trade.

E-commerce and trade in fakes at a first glance

This section of the chapter looks to find observable patterns between e-commerce and illicit trade. To do this, the datasets will be used to calculate the degree of positive correlation between online purchase indicators and global seizures data.

Overall there is a positive and statistically significant correlation between the indicators of e-commerce activity in an economy, and imports of counterfeits to that economy. A positive and statistically robust relation is observed, no matter what proxy of e-commerce is used.

The results of the quantitative exercises are presented in figures below.

Figure 3.1. Proxy of online purchases (in log) and number of customs seizures (in log), 2019

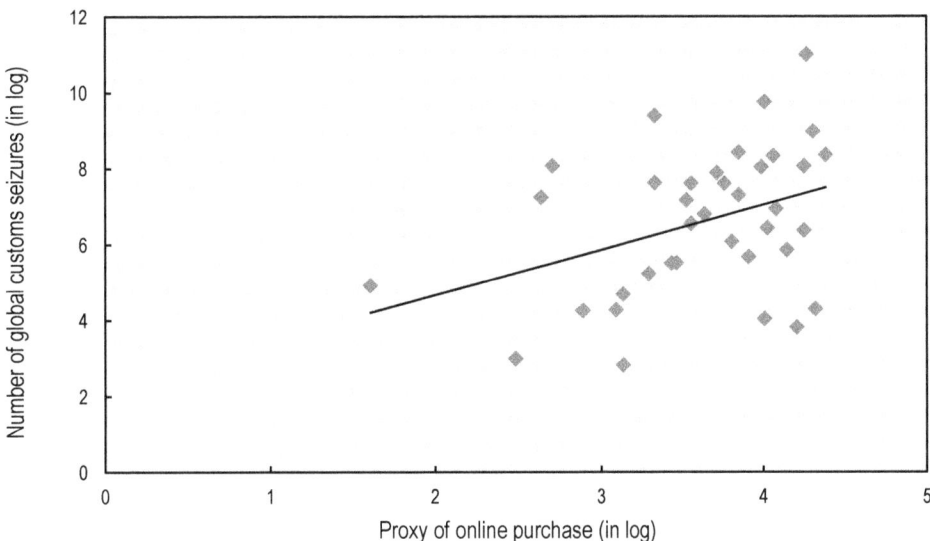

Notes: Only European countries included, and each point corresponds to one European country for 2019; e-commerce activity is represented by "share of individuals who have purchased a good or service online during the prior three months" as reported by Eurostat.
The estimated value of the intercept is 2.30 (1.82) and of the coefficient of the proxy of online purchase (in log) is 1.186 (0.49). The multiple $R^2 = 0.373$
Source: Eurostat ICT Survey on Access and Usage and OECD customs seizures database

Shown by the figure, a relationship between the online purchase proxy and the number of customs seizures is visible. These data point at clear correlation between e-commerce and imports of counterfeit goods to an economy.

Figure 3.2. Proxy of online purchases (in log) and value of customs seizures (in log), 2019

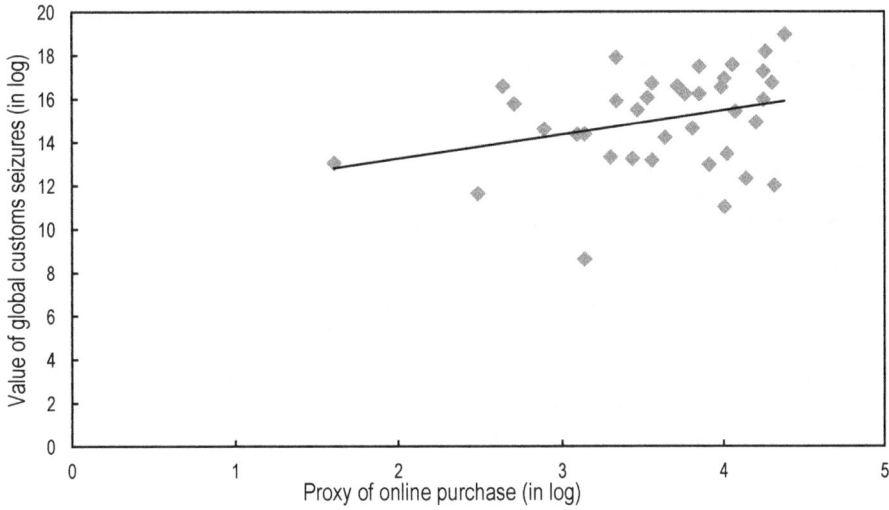

Note: Only European countries included, and each point corresponds to one European country for 2019; e-commerce activity is represented by "share of individuals who have purchased a good or service online during the prior three months" as reported by Eurostat.
The estimated value of the intercept is 11.03 (2.18) and of the coefficient of the proxy of online purchase (in log) is 1.11 (0.59). The multiple $R^2 = 0.3$
Source: Eurostat ICT Survey on Access and Usage and OECD customs seizures database.

Like in the previous data, this figure, which compares e-commerce and the value of counterfeit trade, presents a correlation between online purchase and European illicit trade. A robust, positive correlation appears to be distinguishable, re-confirming the positive correlation between the e-commerce activity in an economy and imports of counterfeits to that economy.

Figure 3.3. Proxy of online purchase (in log) and number of global customs seizures (in log), 2017

Note: Each point corresponds to one economy in 2017. E-commerce activity approximated by the World Bank Global Findex. The estimated value of the intercept is 1.75 (0.83) and of the coefficient of the proxy of online purchase (in log) is 1.05 (0.25). The multiple $R^2 = 0.48$
Source: World Bank Global Findex data and OECD customs seizures database.

Shown in this figure, our proxy of online purchase is positively correlated to the illicit trade indicator. With that said, the correlation between the e-commerce proxy and the trade indicator is stronger than similar indicators from Eurostat, which suggests that e-commerce might be a greater determinant of counterfeit trade when looking at a larger, and more heterogeneous sample of economies, than the European Union only. The finding that countries that do not have developed e-commerce market also do not report large volumes of seizures of fakes, re-iterates the claim of e-commerce being an important solution effectively abused by counterfeiters.

Figure 3.4. Proxy of online purchase (in log) and value of global customs seizures (in log), 2017

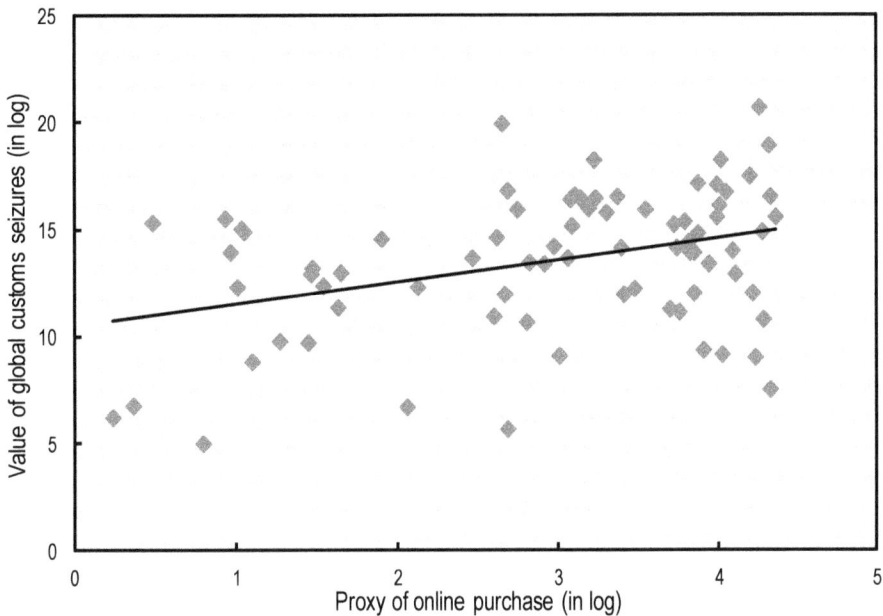

Source: World Bank Global Findex data and OECD customs seizures database.

Like the previous figure, this figure, which compares e-commerce and illicit trade proxies, presents a correlation that seem to be statistically stronger than the one found using Eurostat information, and limited to European countries only. Although the correlation found here is not as distinguishable as the one in the previous figure, the relationship uncovered by the World Bank is stronger than the relationship established using Eurostat data.

Figure 3.5. E-commerce Index and number of global customs seizures (in log), 2019

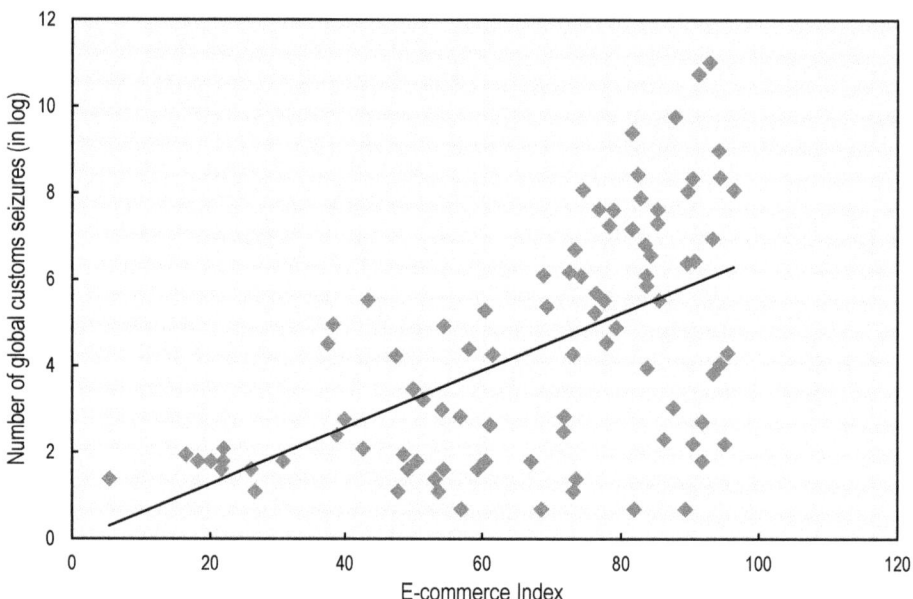

Note: Each point corresponds to one country in 2019. E-commerce activity approximated by UNCTAD E-commerce Index.
The estimated value of the intercept is 46.17 (3.83) and of the coefficient of the number of customs seizures (in log) is 4.79 (0.75). The multiple R^2 = 0.56
Source: UNCTAD E-commerce Index and OECD customs seizures database.

As shown in this figure, the E-commerce index is evidently correlated to global customs seizures data. Supporting the hypothesis created using World Bank data, there appears to be a stronger correlation between e-commerce and illicit trade globally when compared to the European Union. It also suggests that when looking at a broader set of economies, the "effect of e-commerce" (i.e. strong correlation of seizures and e-commerce activity) is clearly visible. It points at e-commerce being an important way of getting to a customer used by counterfeiters.

Figure 3.6. E-commerce Index and value of global customs seizures (in log), 2019

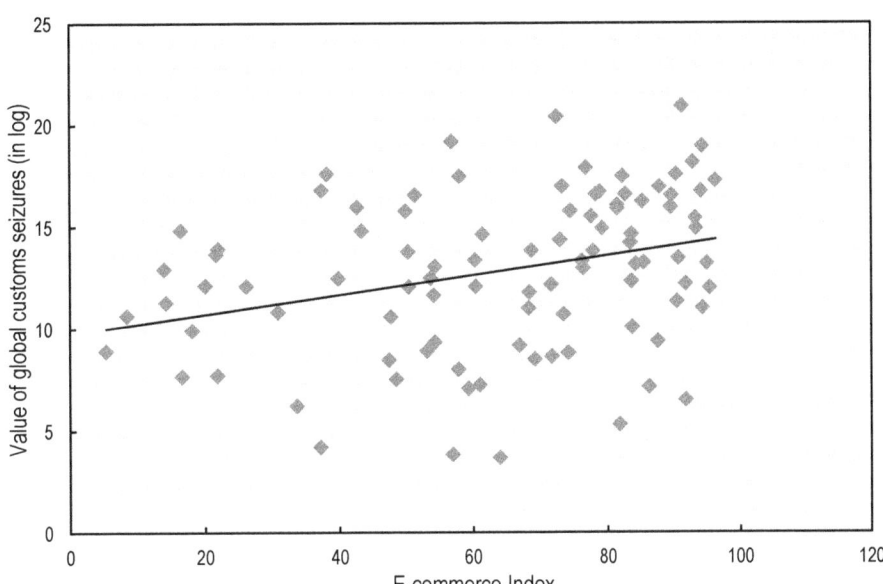

Note: Each point corresponds to one country in 2019. E-commerce activity approximated by UNCTAD E-commerce Index.
The estimated value of the intercept is 9.75 (1.06) and of the coefficient of the E-commerce index is 0.048 (0.015). The multiple $R^2 = 0.3$
Source: UNCTAD E-commerce Index and OECD customs seizures database.

This figure presents a clear correlation between e-commerce and seizure data, although the relationship seems to be weaker. Even though the results seem to be weaker as for other exercises using UNCTAD data, the correlation is still comparable to previously explored e-commerce and illicit trade correlation data.

These six quantitative exercises were conducted for all counterfeit customs seizures in all means of transport. The results from this regression analysis show a positive correlation between various e-commerce proxies and illicit trade indicators. This result suggests that e-commerce does play a role in the global illicit trade landscape, but further analysis is needed to better understand the magnitude of the problem.

In addition, these results point that the problem of abuse of e-commerce by counterfeiters is more pronounced in developed economies, such as the EU. In those economies, consumers often use e-commerce enjoying the flexibility it offers. Unfortunately, criminals abuse these preferences and to a great degree misuse e-commerce as a way to access the market with counterfeits.

Focus on small parcels

The rest of this chapter will analyse trends relating to e-commerce indicators and illicit trade seizures found in small parcels. Since small parcels tend to be the preferred mode of transportation for e-commerce orders, additional checks to link small parcel illicit trade and e-commerce would be useful to develop a heightened understanding of e-commerce and illicit trade. The same three datasets will be used to calculate correlations between these data points, although this section will specifically focus on customs seizures by mail and express couriers (EC).

Figure 3.7. Proxy of online purchase in European countries (in log) and number of customs seizures by mail and EC (in log)

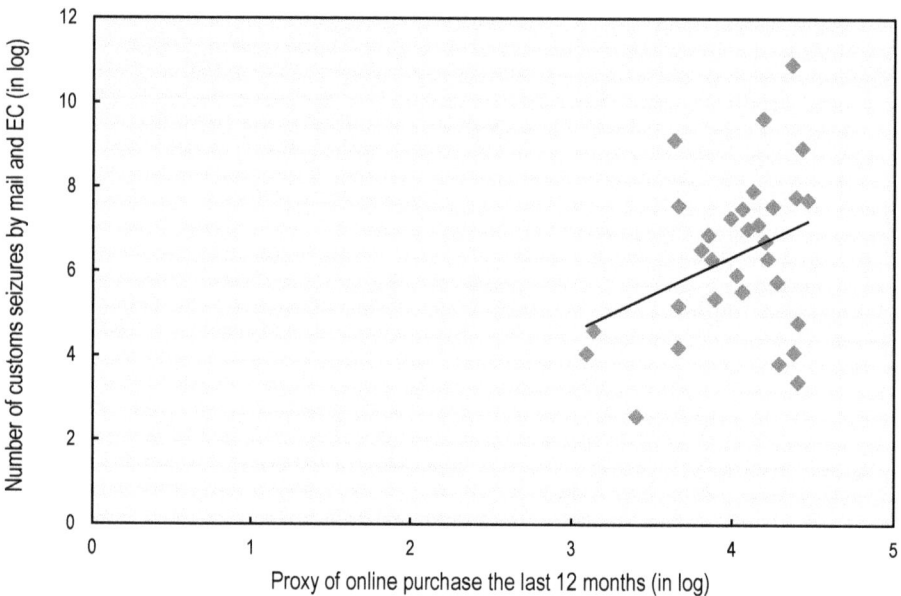

Note: Each point corresponds to one European country in 2019
The estimated value of the coefficient of the proxy of online purchases in the last 12 months (in log) is 1.8 (0.91). The multiple R^2 = 0.34
Source: Eurostat ICT Survey on Access and Usage and OECD customs seizures database.

The observations in this figure differ from the previously analysed Eurostat data by changing the scope of the survey results from 3 months to 12 months and specifying that the counterfeit goods were transported by mail and express and courier services. In the same manner as previous Eurostat information, when the e-commerce proxy is compared to illicit trade indicators, a positive correlation is found between the two factors. This clearly supports the claim that most fakes ordered online are shipped via small parcels.

Figure 3.8. Proxy of online purchase in European countries (in log) and the value of customs seizures by mail and EC (in log)

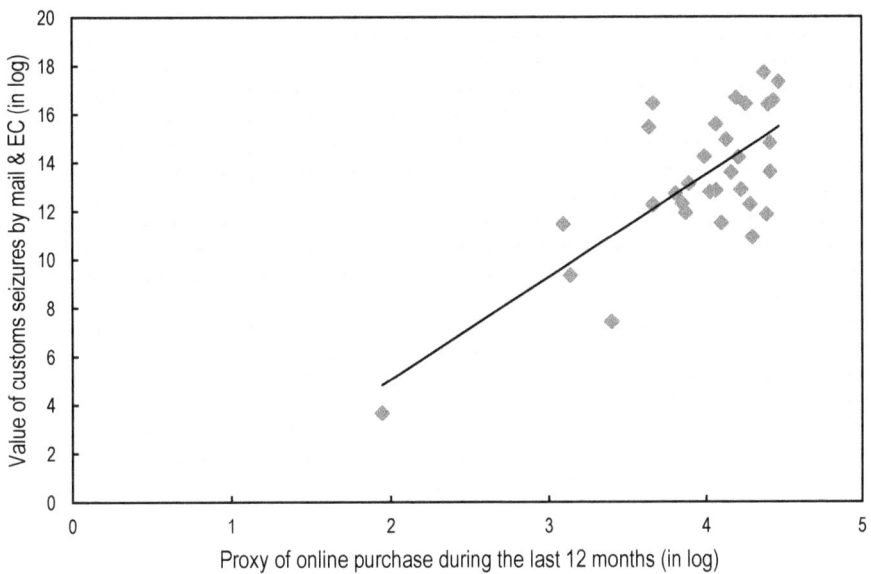

Note: Each point corresponds to one European country in 2019
The estimated value of the coefficient of the proxy of online purchases in the last 12 months (in log) is 4.23 (0.7). The multiple R^2 = 0.74
Source: Eurostat ICT Survey on Access and Usage and OECD customs seizures database.

This figure uses the same proxy of e-commerce as in the last example but combines that data with the value of regional customs seizures by mail and EC, rather than the quantity. When making this comparison, an evident trend emerges. This figure provides a clear correlation between e-commerce and illicit trade. And since this relationship is strong, a significant positive correlation between online purchase and the value of customs seizures by small parcels is justifiable.

Figure 3.9. Proxy of online purchase (in log) and number of global customs seizures by mail & express courier

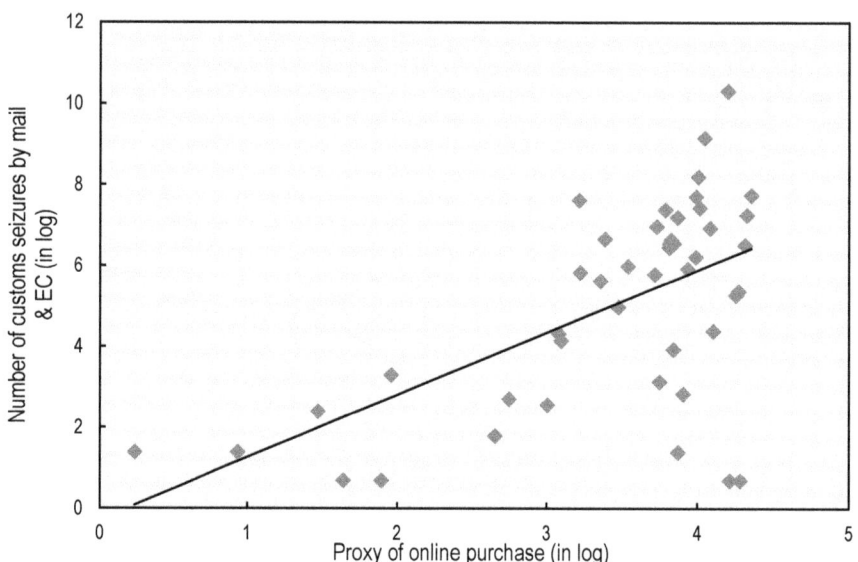

Note: Each point corresponds to one country in 2017
The estimated value of the coefficient of the proxy of online purchase is 1.54 (0.33). The multiple R^2 = 0.58
Source: World Bank Global Findex data and OECD customs seizures database.

The correlations presented in this figure point at a clear links between World Bank index of online purchase and global seizures. Continuing the trends discovered from previous observations, the World Bank correlation is stronger than the comparable Eurostat correlation. Put it differently, looking at a larger set of countries, including those, where e-commerce is used less intensely, one sees a much clearer correlation between the degree of seizures and e-commerce intensity. For the EU-only the correlation is less visible, as e-commerce is popular in the EU, and hence most European countries are more intensely targeted by counterfeiters that abuse the on-line environment.

Figure 3.10. Proxy of online purchase (in log) and number of global customs seizures by mail & express courier

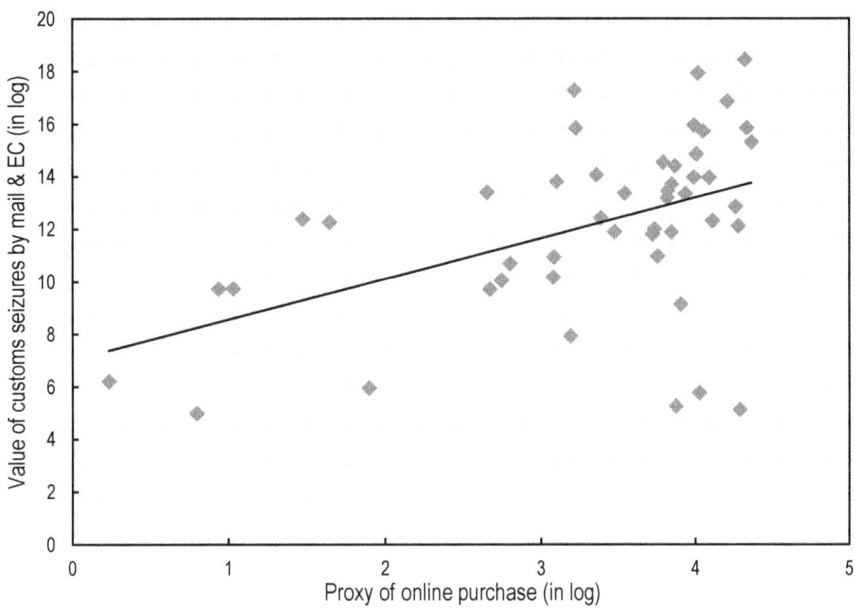

Note: Each point corresponds to one country in 2017
The estimated value of the intercept is 7.01 (1.49) and of the coefficient of the proxy of online purchase (in log) is 1.54 (0.43). The multiple $R^2 = 0.46$
Source: World Bank Global Findex data and OECD customs seizures database.

When using the World Bank proxy of e-commerce and the value of global customs seizure by mail and EC, the correlation peculiarly weakens. Since this identical comparison presented the strongest correlation using Eurostat data, it could be assumed that this comparison would yield the strongest relationship for World Bank data as well. In fact, breaking from the previously observed pattern, the World Bank figure showed a weaker correlation than the comparable one based on the Eurostat data.

Figure 3.11. E-commerce Index and number of global customs seizures (in log)

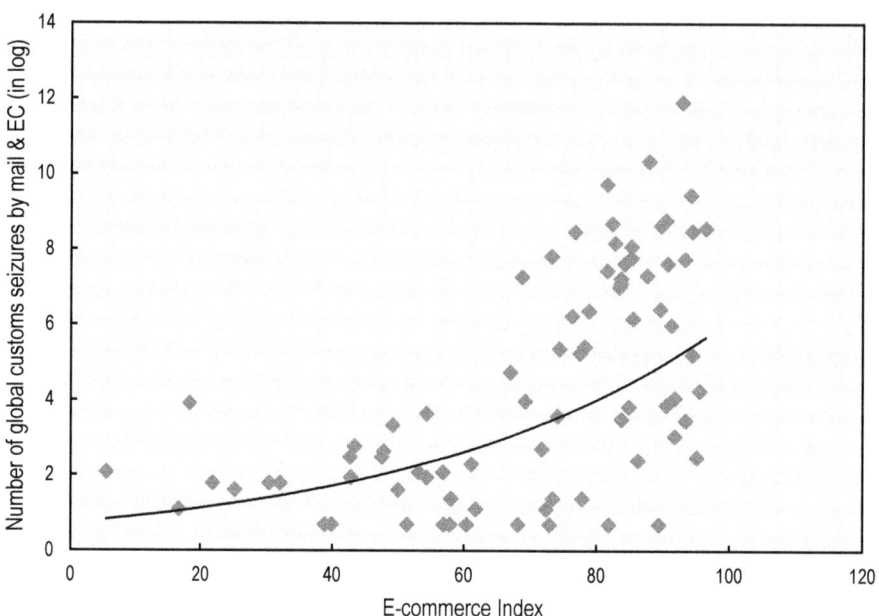

Note: Each point corresponds to one country in 2019
The estimated value of the coefficient of the E-commerce index is 0.08 (0.012). The multiple R^2 = 0.59
Source: UNCTAD E-commerce Index and OECD customs seizures database.

The correlation depicted in this figure between the UNCTAD E-commerce index and the global illicit trade indicator is quite strong. Clearly shown by the figure, the data follows the constructed regression line and present a clear positive correlation between e-commerce and global illicit trade in small parcels. In fact, this comparison of the E-commerce index on the number of global customs seizures by mail and express courier (EC) is the strongest correlation observed using UNCTAD information.

Figure 3.12. E-commerce Index and value of global customs seizures (in log)

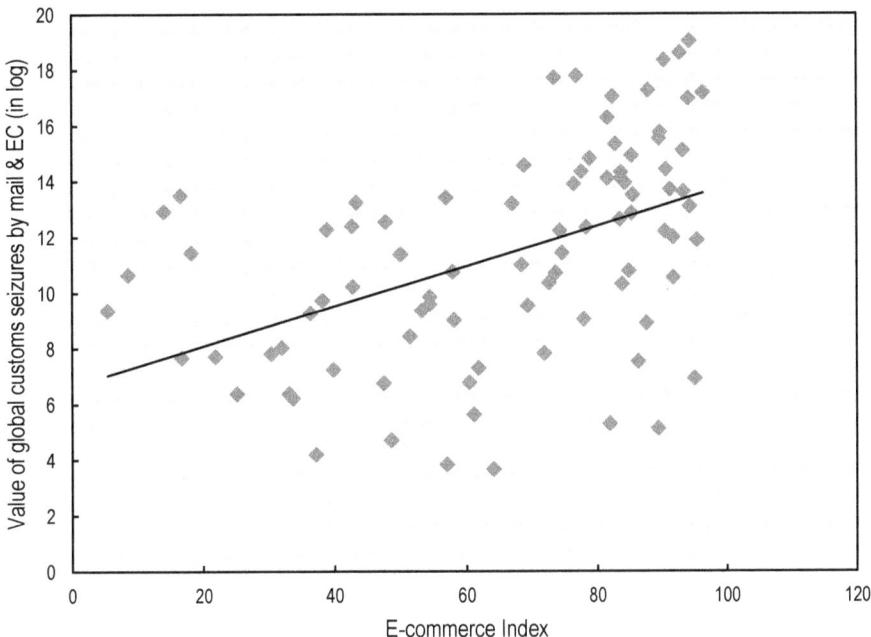

Note: Each point corresponds to one country in 2019
The estimated value of the coefficient of the E-commerce index is 0.07 (0.014). The multiple R^2 = 0.46
Source: UNCTAD E-commerce Index and OECD customs seizures database.

The final check, based on UNCTAD data and shown in this figure, presents a moderate correlation between the e-commerce index and the value of global seizures by mail and EC. The result from this dataset was similar to the result from the World Bank dataset. This finding makes sense since both analyses capture world data, compared to Eurostat which uses regional data, for e-commerce proxies and compares it to the same set of customs seizures.

Comparing the regressions between overall customs seizures and customs seizures by mail and EC, an interesting trend emerges. Each correlation involving small parcels is either similar or more significant than the corresponding correlation reached in the overall seizure section. This finding suggests that e-commerce has noticeable impacts in increasing trade in counterfeits since small parcels are the predominant mode of transportation for e-commerce deliveries.

Moreover, this pattern is particularly strong for developed economies, such as the EU. As e-commerce is popular in the EU, most European countries are intensely targeted by counterfeiters that abuse the on-line environment, and use small parcels as the conveyance method.

References

Amazon (2021), *Brand Protection Report*, https://assets.aboutamazon.com/96/a0/90f229d54c8cba5072b2c4e021f7/amz-brand-report.pdf. [41]

Andrenelli, A. (2019), "Electronic transmissions and international trade - shedding new light on the moratorium debate", *OECD Trade Policy Papers*, Vol. 233, https://doi.org/10.1787/57b50a4b-en. [16]

DHS (2020), *Combating Trafficking in Counterfeit and Pirated Goods*, US Department of Homeland Security, Washington, https://www.dhs.gov/sites/default/files/publications/20_0124_plcy_counterfeit-pirated-goods-report_01.pdf. [32]

eBay (2021), *2020 Global Transparency Report*, http://www.ebaymainstreet.com/sites/default/files/2021-05/2020-eBay-Global-Transparency-Report.pdf. [40]

EC (2017), *Overview of the functioning of the Memorandum of Understanding on the sale of counterfeit goods via the internet, SWD(2017) 430 final*, https://ec.europa.eu/docsroom/documents/26602. [30]

EC (2016), *Memorandum of Understanding: 21 June 2016, Ref. Ares(2016)3934515 26/07/2016*, European Commission, Brussels, https://ec.europa.eu/docsroom/documents/43321/attachments/2/translations/en/renditions/native. [29]

EC (2013), *Report from the Commission to the European Parliament and the Council on the Functioning of the Memorandum of Understanding on the Sale of Counterfeit Goods via the Internet, COM(2013), 209 final,*, European Commission, Brussels,, http://Ref. Ares(2016). [28]

EC (2020b), *Report on the functioning of the Memorandum of Understanding on the sale of Counterfeit Goods on the internet, SWD(2020) 166 final/2*, European Commission, Brussels, https://ec.europa.eu/docsroom/documents/42701. [27]

EUIPO (2021), *Monitoring and analysing social media in relation to IPR infringement Report*, https://euipo.europa.eu/tunnel-web/secure/webdav/guest/document_library/observatory/documents/reports/2021_Monitoring_and_analysing_social_media_in_relation_to_IPR_Infringement_Report/2021_Monitoring_and_analysing_social_media_in_relation_to_IPR_Infringem. [20]

EUIPO (2021), *New and existing trends in using social media for IP infringement activities and good practices to address them*, https://euipo.europa.eu/tunnel-web/secure/webdav/guest/document_library/observatory/documents/reports/2021_Social_Media/2021_Social_Media_Discussion_Paper_FullR_en.pdf. [19]

GCIG (2016), *One Internet, Centre for International Governance Innovation and Chatham House*, http://www.cigionline.org/documents/1045/gcig_final_report_-_with_cover.pdf. [39]

Goldberg, S. (2019), "Regulating Privacy Online: An Economic Evaluation of the GDPR", *SSRN Working Paper*, http://dx.doi.org/10.2139/ssrn.3421731. [21]

Group, I. (2020), *IP Crime and Enforcement Report*, IP Crime Group Secretariat, Concept House, Newport, https://assets.publishing.service.gov.uk/government/uploads/system/uploads/attachment_data/file/913644/ip-crime-report-2019-20.pdf. [31]

INTA (2020), *Addressing the Sale of Counterfeits on the Internet*, https://www.inta.org/wp-content/uploads/public-files/advocacy/committee-reports/Addressing_the_Sale_of_Counterfeits_on_the_Internet_June_2021_edit.pdf. [22]

OCDE/EUIPO (2021), *Misuse of Containerized Maritime Shipping in the Global Trade of Counterfeits*, Éditions OCDE, Paris,, https://doi.org/10.1787/e39d8939-en. [9]

OECD (2021), *COVID-19 vaccine and the Threat of Illicit Trade, Chair's Summary Note*, https://www.oecd.org/gov/illicit-trade/summary-note-covid-19-vaccine-and-the-threat-of-illicit-trade.pdf. [35]

OECD (2021), *Illicit trade: Discussions with stakeholders*, unpublished. [26]

OECD (2020), *Illicit Trade in a Time of Crisis. Chair's Summary Note*, https://www.oecd.org/gov/illicit-trade/oecd-webinar-illicit-trade-time-crisis-23-april.pdf. [10]

OECD (2020), *OECD Digital Economy Outlook 2020*, OECD Publishing, Paris, https://doi.org/10.1787/bb167041-en. [11]

OECD (2020), *Trade in Fake Medicines at the Time of the Covid-19 Pandemics. Chair's Summary Note*, https://www.oecd.org/gov/illicit-trade/oecd-fake-medicines-webinar-june-10-summary-note.pdf. [34]

OECD (2018), *Governance Frameworks to Counter Illicit Trade*, OECD Publishing, Paris,, https://doi.org/10.1787/9789264291652-en. [33]

OECD (2011), *OECD Council Recommendation on Principles for Internet Policy Making*, OECD, Paris, https://www.oecd.org/sti/ieconomy/49258588.pdf. [37]

OECD (2008), *The Economic Impact of Counterfeiting and Piracy*, Éditions OCDE, Paris, https://doi.org/10.1787/9789264045521-en. [13]

OECD (2016a), *Ministerial Declaration on the Digital Economy*, OECD, http://www.oecd.org/digital/Digital-Economy-Ministerial-Declaration-2016.pdf. [38]

OECD (2016b), *Recommendation of the Council on Consumer Protection in E-commerce*, OECD, Paris, https://legalinstruments.oecd.org/en/instruments/OECD-LEGAL-0422. [17]

OECD/EUIPO (2021), *Global Trade in Fakes: a Worrying Threat*, OECD Publishing, https://www.oecd.org/publications/global-trade-in-fakes-74c81154-en.htm. [4]

OECD/EUIPO (2020), *Trade in Counterfeit Pharmaceutical Products*, Illicit Trade, OECD Publishing, Paris, https://dx.doi.org/10.1787/a7c7e054-en. [8]

OECD/EUIPO (2019), *Trends in Trade in Counterfeit and Pirated Goods*, OECD Publishing, Paris,, https://doi.org/10.1787/g2g9f533-en. [3]

OECD/EUIPO (2018), *Misuse of Small Parcels for Trade in Counterfeit Goods: Facts and Trends*, OECD Publishing, Paris, https://doi.org/10.1787/9789264307858-en. [7]

OECD/EUIPO (2018), *Trade in Counterfeit Goods and Free Trade Zones: Evidence from Recent Trends*, OECD Publishing, Paris/EUIPO, Alicante, https://doi.org/10.1787/9789264289550-en. [5]

OECD/EUIPO (2018), *Why Do Countries Export Fakes?: The Role of Governance Frameworks, Enforcement and Socio-economic Factors*, OECD Publishing, Paris/EUIPO, Alicante, https://doi.org/10.1787/9789264302464-en. [6]

OECD/EUIPO (2017), *Mapping the Real Routes of Trade in Fake Goods, Illicit Trade*, OECD Publishing, Paris, https://doi.org/10.1787/9789264278349-en. [2]

OECD/EUIPO (2016), *Trade in Counterfeit and Pirated Goods: Mapping the Economic Impact, Illicit Trade*, OECD Publishing, Paris, https://doi.org/10.1787/9789264252653-en. [1]

Phaneuf, A. (2021), *Social Commerce 2021: Social media and Ecommerce Convergence Trends Brings Growth Opportunity for Brands, Insider Inc.*,, http://www.businessinsider.com/social-commerce-brand-trends-marketing-strategies. [18]

S. Goldberg, G. (2019), "Regulating Privacy Online: An Economic Evaluation of the GDPR", *SSRN Working Paper*, http://dx.doi.org/10.2139/ssrn.3421731. [42]

Sorescu, S. (2021), "Trade in the time of parcels", *OECD Trade Policy Papers*, Vol. 249, https://doi.org/10.1787/0faac348-en. [15]

Tian, H. (2018), *Bullet-proof payment processors*, https://ieeexplore.ieee.org/document/8376208. [23]

UNCTAD (2021), *Estimates of global e-commerce 2019 and preliminary assessment of COVID-19 impact on online retail 2020*, United Nations Conference on Trade and Development, Geneva, https://unctad.org/system/files/official-document/tn_unctad_ict4d18_en.pdf. [14]

UNICRI (2020), *"Cyber-crime during the COVID-19 Pandemic"*, http://www.unicri.it/news/cyber-crime-during-covid-19-pandemic. [12]

UPU (2020), *E-commerce Guide*, Universal Postal Union, Berne, https://www.upu.int/UPU/media/upu/publications/Final-November-update-UPU-E-Commerce-Guide_2020_EN.pdf. [25]

USPS (2020/21), *FY 2020 Annual Report to Congress*, United States Postal Service, https://about.usps.com/what/financials/annual-reports/fy2020.pdf. [24]

WCO (2020), *Illicit Trade Report 2019*, WCO, Brussels,, http://www.wcoomd.org/-/media/wco/public/global/pdf/topics/enforcement-and-compliance/activities-and-programmes/illicit-trade-report/itr_2019_en.pdf?db=web. [36]

4 Trade in fakes and e-commerce: Focus on the EU

This chapter presents a deep-dive view of the online trade in counterfeit goods based on EU data. Seizure data provided by the enforcement authorities in the EU indicates if a seizure referred to a good that was ordered online. Such information permits carrying out a detailed assessment of types of fake products ordered on-line, specific transport modes abused and the provenance economies of these goods to the EU.

Seizures related to online transactions

Some seizures registered by custom offices of the EU Member States contain information that they were related to online sales of goods. The link with online sale of goods is determined by custom officers on a case by case basis, considering documentation accompanying the shipped goods.

In practice there is wide heterogeneity between EU Member States as regards provision of this information. Whereas in some countries the majority of the detentions are associated with online sale, in other countries no single seizure has been associated with online sales of goods in the entire period of 2017-2019. To reduce the impact of this heterogeneity on the analysis, data from countries which do not report any detentions related to online sales or where the share of detentions related to online sales is lower than 5% have been eliminated from further analysis.

As could be seen on Figure 4.1 the detentions related to online sales constitute majority of all the seizure observations registered between 2017 and 2019.

Figure 4.1. Distribution of detentions between online sales and detentions not related to online sales

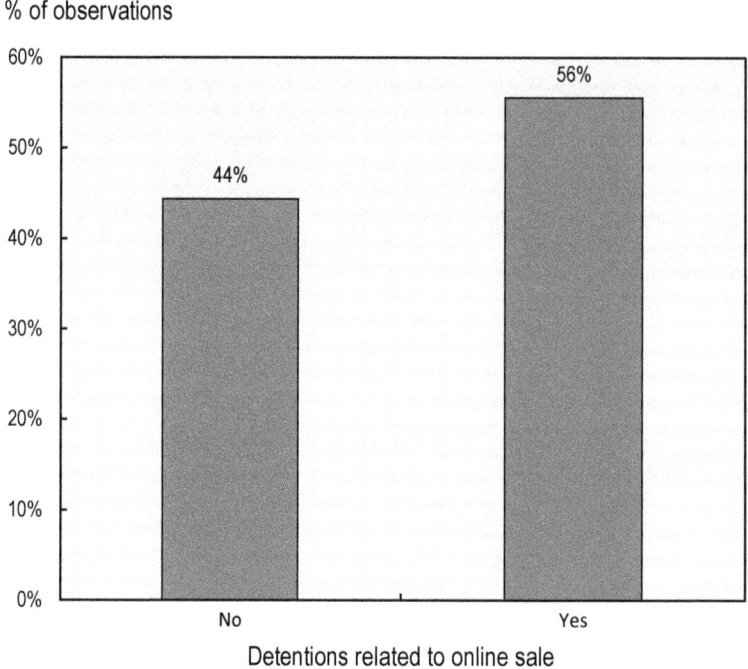

Source: OECD/EUIPO

However, as shown on Figure 4.2, value of counterfeit goods, not related to online sales is still much higher than value of seized counterfeit goods, for which the link with internet sale could be established.

Figure 4.2. Distribution of value of seizures between online sales and detentions not related to online sales

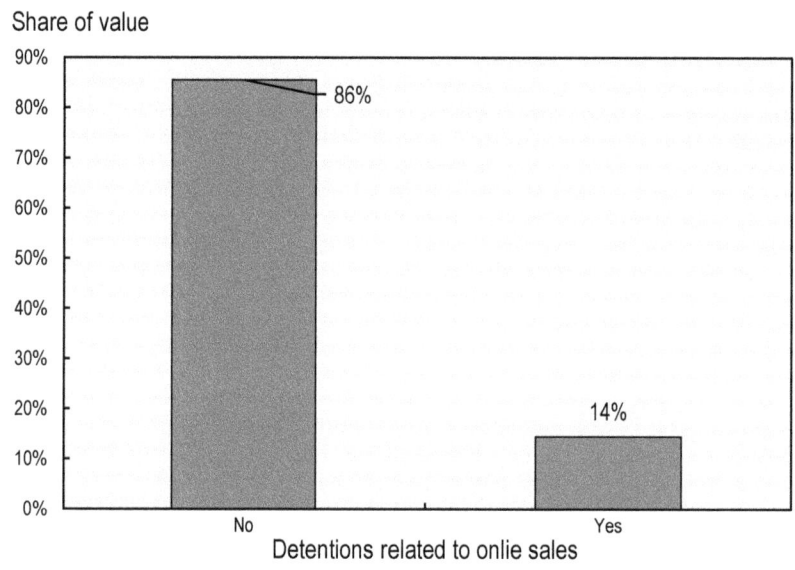

Source: OECD/EUIPO

Transport modes

As could be expected, there is a large difference in the modes of transport being used to ship counterfeit products purchased online and products not related with online sale.

Figure 4.3. Distribution of detentions between transport modes

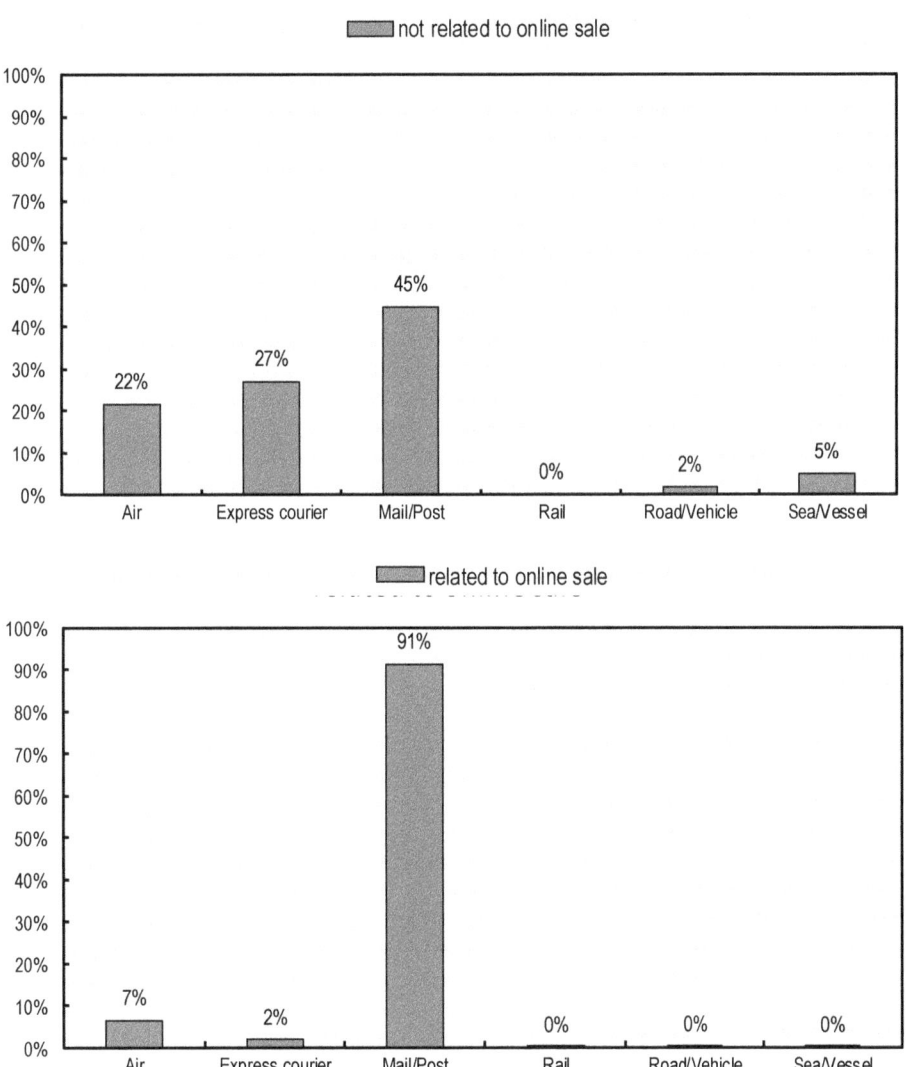

Source: OECD/EUIPO

Mail/post transport mode dominates in terms of number of detention cases, irrespective whether the sale of counterfeit goods has been performed online. In the case of online sales however, mail is associated with over 90% of detentions. All other modes of transport play by far less important role in the online sale of counterfeit goods than in case of shipment of counterfeit goods not related to online sale. Air transport is the second most important transport mode associated with online sale of counterfeit goods. Its share in detentions of goods related to online sales amounts to 6.6%. Share of all other transport modes in total number of detentions related to online sales is slightly higher than 2%.

As seen in Figure 4.4 mail/post is the only transport mode of counterfeit goods where the number of detentions related with online sale is higher than the number of cases not related to online sale. The share of seizures identified as related to online sales by custom officers is as high as 72%. In the case of any other transport mode, the share of cases related with online sale is much lower and does not exceed 30%, with the share as low as 1.5% in case of maritime transport.

Figure 4.4. Share of detentions related to online sales within each transport mode (online and not online=100%)

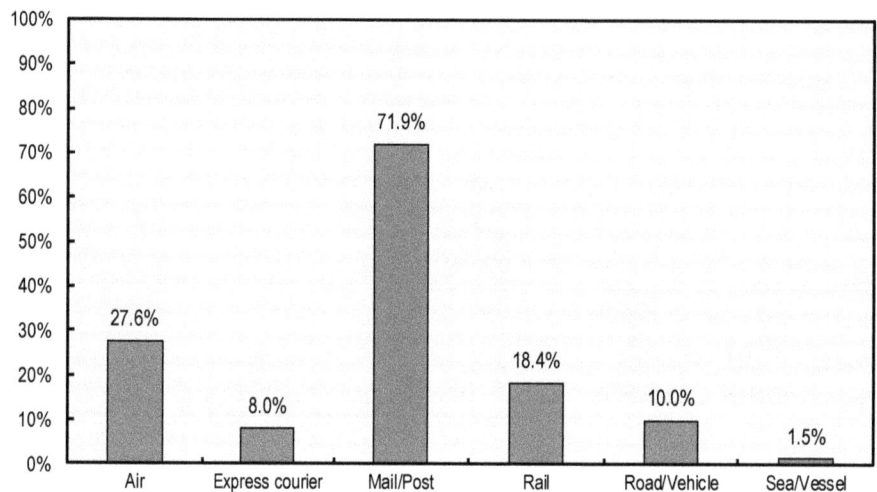

Source: OECD/EUIPO

Statistics on the transport modes and value of the counterfeit goods shown in Figure 4.5 suggest similar dominant role of mail in transnational shipment of counterfeit goods purchased online. Unlike in cases of seizure not related to online sales of counterfeit goods, where the maritime transport plays a dominant role, in case of online sales, over 80% of value of seized goods is related to transport by mail. Comparison of Figure 4.3 and Figure 4.5 shows that air transport and, in particular, express courier shipments' shares in total value of seized goods related to online sales are bigger than their respective shares in total number of detentions. It may indicate that counterfeit items of higher value purchased online outside of the EU tend to be shipped more frequently by air and express courier in comparison to less expensive counterfeit goods, which tend to be shipped by post.

Figure 4.5. Distribution of value of counterfeit goods between transport modes

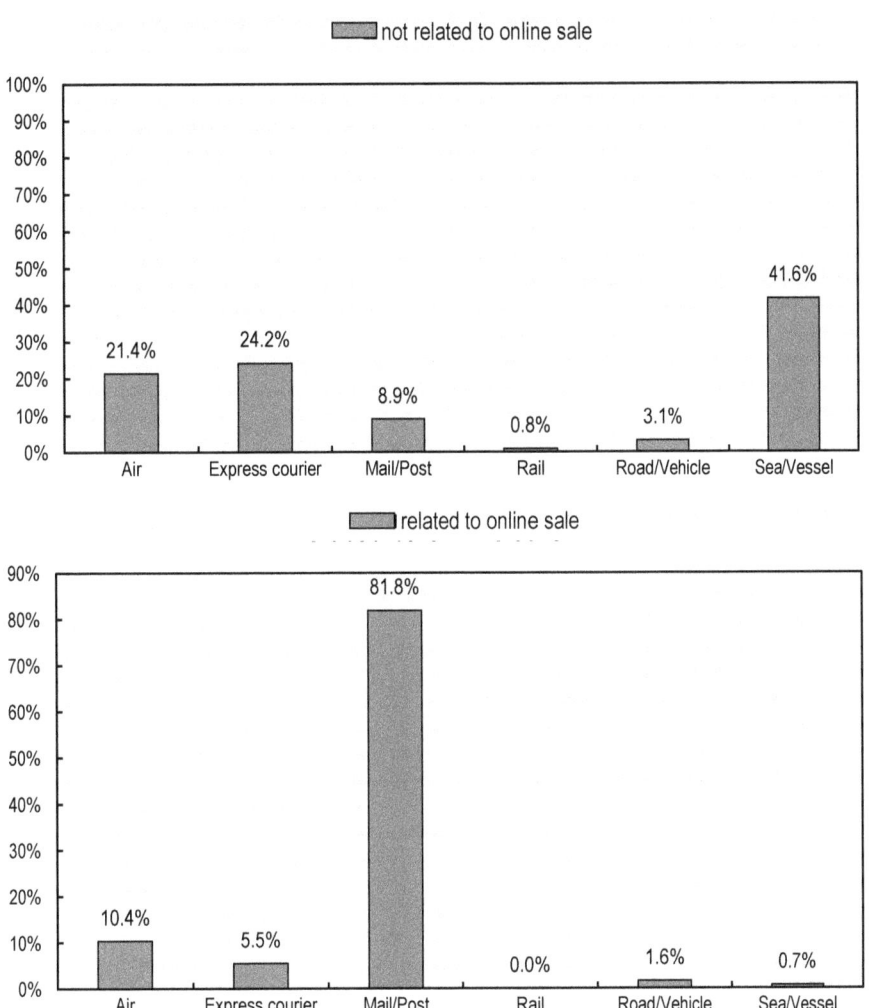

Source: OECD/EUIPO.

Overall dominance of the maritime transport for shipments not related to online sales of goods and relatively low value of goods related with online transactions and seized on the EU borders may indicate that the direct customer online purchase of counterfeit goods from distributors with seat outside of the EU still plays the minor role in the import of counterfeit goods into the EU. Prevalent modus operandi seems to be the wholesale purchase of counterfeit goods or components necessary to their assembly by distributors located inside the EU and their subsequent retail distribution on the physical or online marketplaces. Shipment of goods ordered via ecommerce platforms from third countries and transported to fulfillment centers in the EU in packages stacked in containers is a relatively new phenomenon detected by custom officers. This may lead to the underestimation of the role of ecommerce in the delivery of counterfeit goods to final consumers in the EU, as it is very difficult for custom officers to detect counterfeits in containers packed in this manner.

Provenance economies

As shown in Figure 4.6 and Figure 4.7 the ranking of provenance countries of the counterfeit goods for purchases not related to Internet and those with a link to online sale are similar. However, the role of China is even more pronounced in case of transactions performed online. China was a provenance country for over 75% of detentions with a link to online sale, whereas in case of transactions not indicated as related to Internet sale, its share in detentions is below 50%. Singapore, US, Malaysia and India play also more important role as provenance countries for counterfeit goods purchased online than those not related to online transactions.

Figure 4.6. Provenance countries of seizures not related to online sales (share of detentions)

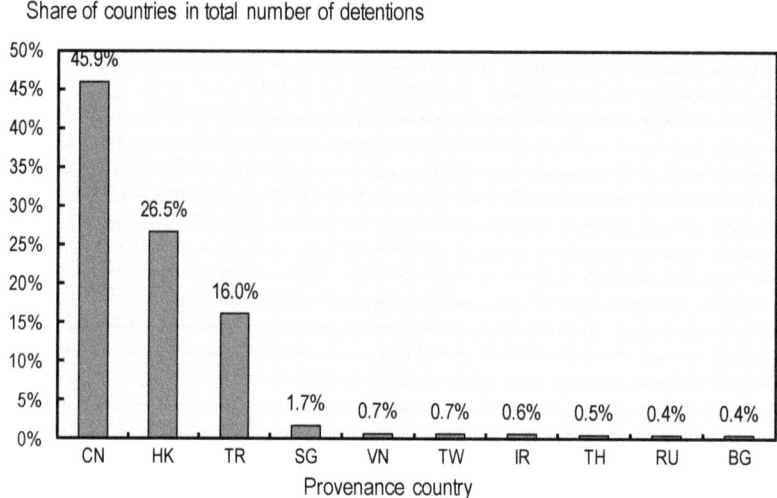

Source: OECD/EUIPO.

Figure 4.7. Provenance countries of seizures related to online sales (share of detentions)

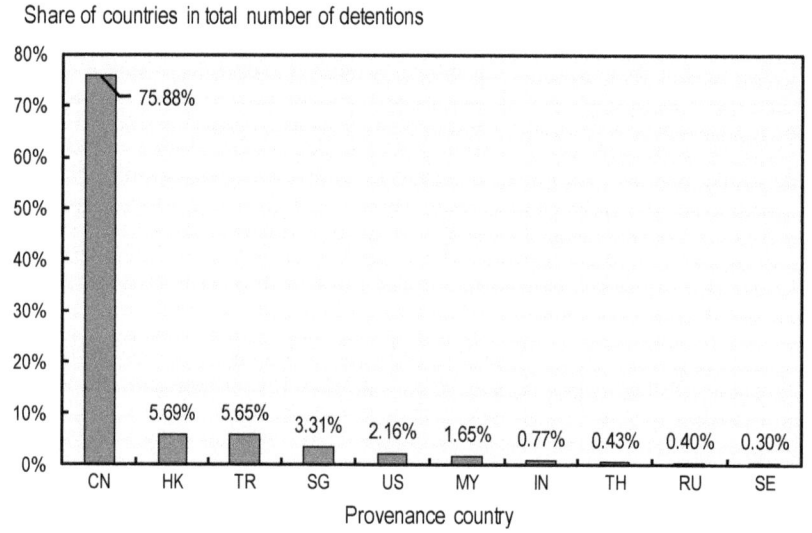

Source: OECD/EUIPO.

China is also a dominant provenance country in terms of value of counterfeit goods purchased online. The share of value of counterfeit goods shipped from China is slightly below 70% of total value of counterfeit goods purchased online.

Figure 4.8. Provenance countries of seizures not related to online sales (value of seized goods)

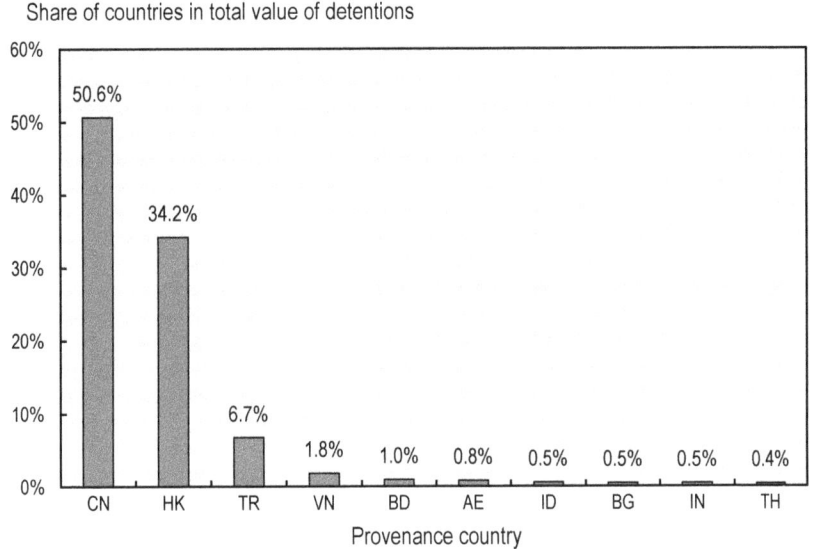

Source: OECD/EUIPO.

Figure 4.9. Provenance countries of seizures related to online sales (value of seized goods)

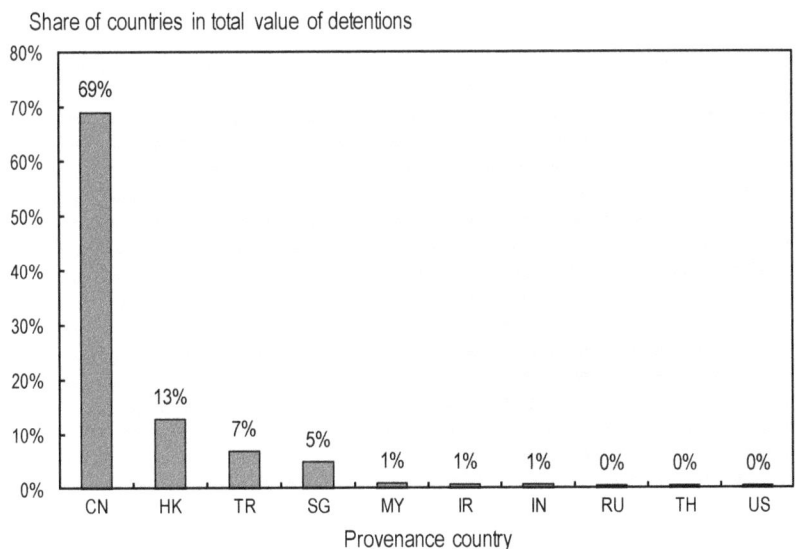

Source: OECD/EUIPO.

Types of fakes purchased online

Many types of fake products tend to be ordered on-line including footwear, clothes, toys, leather goods, electrical equipment and watches and cosmetics.

Figure 4.10. Distribution of number of detentions not related to online sales between product categories

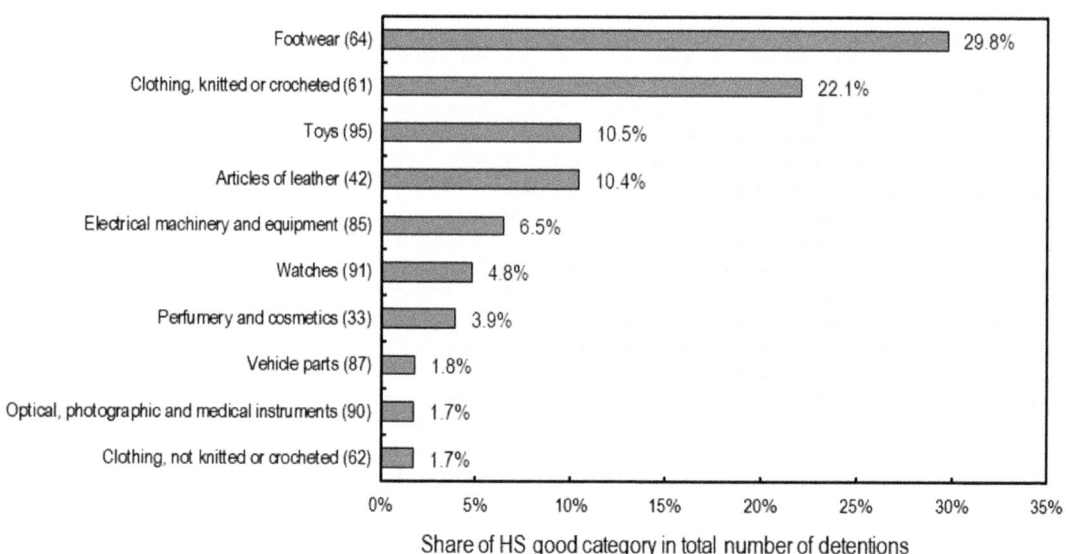

Source: OECD/EUIPO.

Figure 4.11. Distribution of number of detentions related to online sales between product categories

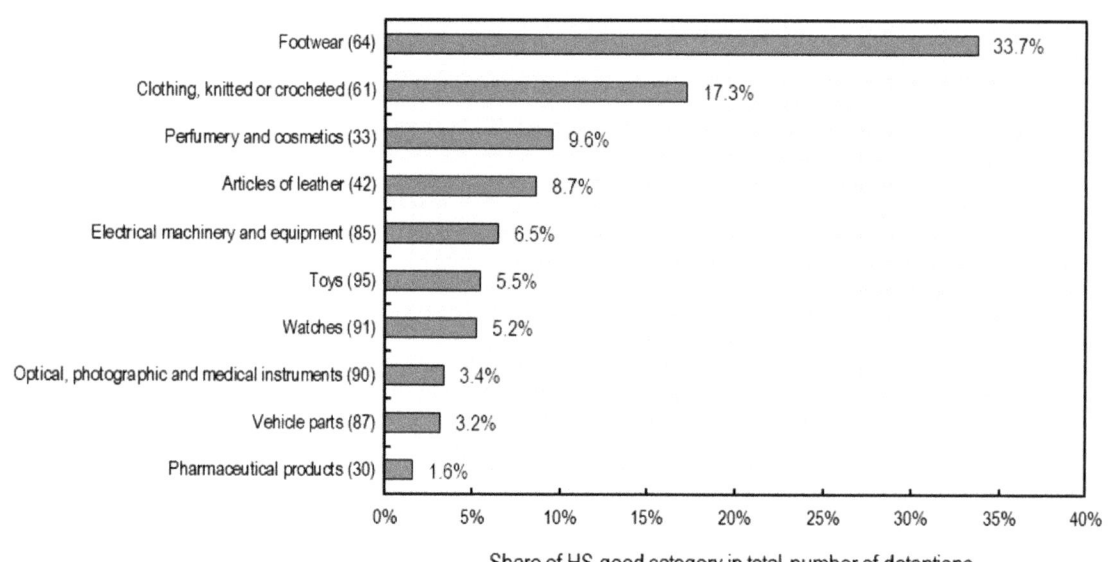

Source: OECD/EUIPO.

Figure 4.11 present the distribution of the detentions between product categories, in the context of online and non-online purchases. Two rankings are quite similar, with footwear and clothing being product categories on top of the list of products with highest shares of detentions. However, some changes in the composition of rankings indicates that the share of shipments related to online sales differs depending on the product category. This intuition is confirmed in the Figure 4.12 which shows the ranking of counterfeit products sorted by the share of detentions related to online purchase. As could be seen in that Figure, for three categories of products: Perfumery and cosmetics, Pharmaceutical products and optical products (glasses) the share of detentions related to online purchases exceeded 70%. In case of vehicle parts, footwear and watches the share of detentions related to online sale of goods is also higher than the average for the entire dataset of detentions.

Figure 4.12. Share of detentions related to online sales by good category (by number of detentions)

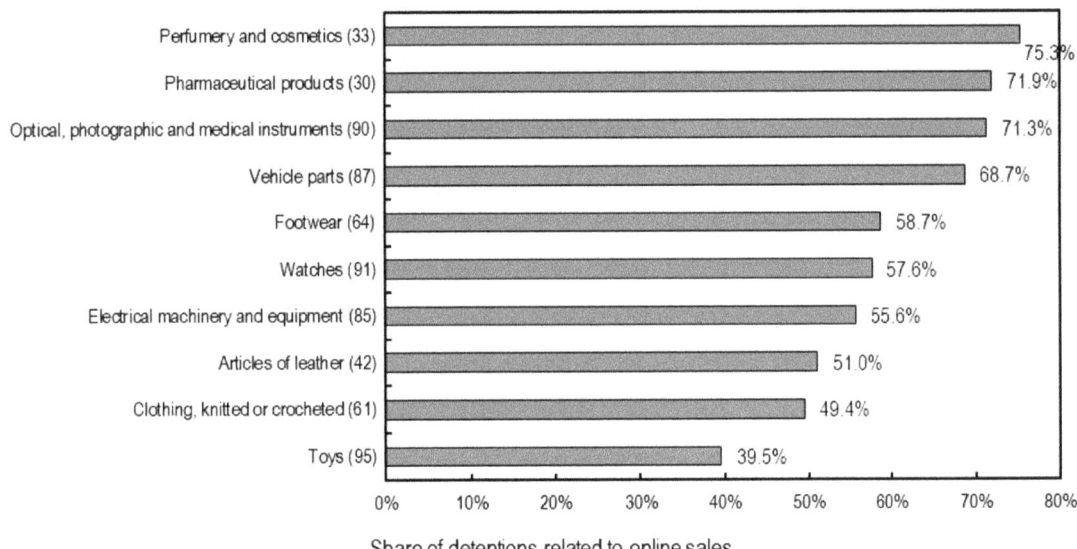

Note: top 10 goods' categories by number of cases; online and non-online transactions in each product category =100%
Source: OECD/EUIPO.

As could be expected, the share of detentions related to online sales in almost every product category is lower when measured by value then when measured by number of detentions. It is a result of the negative correlation between the share of detentions related to online sale of goods and the mean number of items transported using given mode of transport. It is reflected in Figure 4.13 which shows the share of value of seized products related to online transactions within each product category. Still, for three product categories: vehicles parts, pharmaceutical products and watches the value of seized counterfeit products purchased online exceeded 20% of value of all products seized within their respective categories. The value of counterfeit products related to online purchase is also higher than average for jewellery and articles of leather.

Figure 4.13. Share of detentions related to online sales by good category (by value of seized articles)

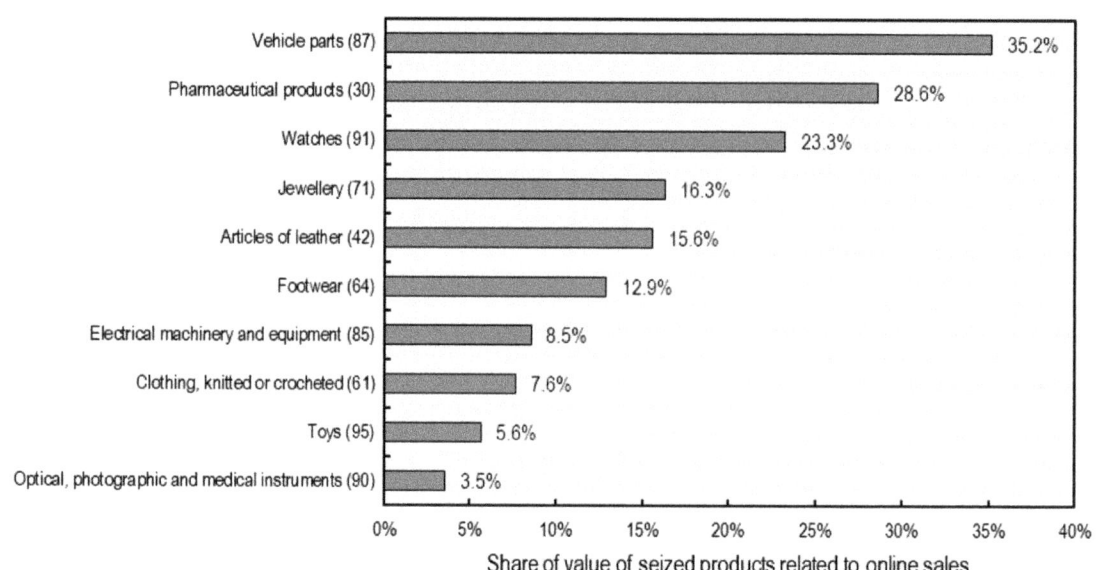

Note: top 10 goods' categories by number of cases; online and non-online transactions in each product category =100%
Source: OECD/EUIPO.

5 Governance frameworks

This section sketches governance frameworks to counter proliferations of counterfeits developed either by public authorities, and some best practices developed by the on-line industry. It explores the different roles that government is playing with respect to governance and the actions that some are taking to address certain issues in their jurisdictions, and the efforts that some of the largest market platform operators are making to enhance the trust of sellers and buyers alike in their platforms.

In many jurisdictions, policymakers have recognized challenges related to proliferation of counterfeit goods in the e-commerce environment. The risks posed by counterfeits online for consumers, innovation and the damages it can cause to the economy are vital threat that is being addressed by policymakers in a number of ways. Actions focused on precise regulations, consumer protection, streamlining of liability, enhancement of cross-industry co-operation etc.

Industry has been also active in this area, and developed a number of best practices, and efforts. There are many examples of mechanisms to flag the presence of fake goods on online platform, to resolve disputes between sellers and consumers in a fair and timely manner, or to ensure that platforms' terms and conditions includes their commitment not to sell counterfeit products.

Government-led measures

In many jurisdictions, governments have been active in addressing issues concerning bad actors and e-commerce fraud in recent years, in a variety of ways, by encouraging co-operation with and among stakeholders, and through specific initiatives designed to improve the functioning of e-commerce.[1]

Australia

In Australia, a pilot project is underway which seeks to authenticate the merchandise being sold on a platform (OECD, 2021[26]). In 2019, IP Australia, the government agency which is responsible for administering intellectual property (IP) rights and legislation relating to patents, trademarks, designs and plant breeder's rights,[2] developed a Smart Trade Mark mechanism, which is designed to help business and consumers determine whether the products that they are purchasing are authentic (i.e. not counterfeit), using block chain technology. The system enables trademark holders to request IP Australia to attach a business-critical artefact, which in the case of Smart Trade Mark is a URL, to the government's trademark registry. The link can then be verified using Amazon's Quantum Ledger Database (QLDB) service.[3]

European Union

In the European Union key governance actions to counter the abuse of e-commerce in trade in counterfeit goods are centred at the European Commission, and the EU Agencies, such as the EUIPO. The key initiative is the *Memorandum of Understanding (MoU) on the Sale of Counterfeit Goods on the Internet* facilitated by the European Commission. In addition, the EU considers two pieces of legislation in the e-commerce area: the Digital Markets Act (DMA) and the Digital Services Act (DSA). Last, the EUIPO administers and implements some specific systems, including implementation of the MoU.

Apart from the European Commission and the EU Agencies, EU member states were also taking governance actions to address this risk. An illustrative example are measures taken by Belgium (Box 5.1).

> ### Box 5.1. Governance measures in Belgium
>
> In Belgium, counterfeiting levels remain high, but there has been progress in fighting the problem, reflecting the success of the operation In Our Sites (IOS) which was carried out in co-operation with Europol in 2018, with the support of FPS Economy, EURid, DNS Belgium and customs authorities. In 2019 and 2020, some 990 and 1,016 sites, respectively, were shut down. While the number of closures edged upward, it did not match the significant growth in online sales during the pandemic, which is seen as a positive sign.
>
> The Belgian approach has been a proactive one, with increased attention being paid to registration procedures. Until recently it was relatively simple to set up a domain. After entering basic information, a site would be operational immediately. Once online, applicants would have 14 days to correct any incorrect or fraudulent data, with site closure occurring if no action was taken by the registrant to correct information. With a view towards better protecting consumers and rights holder, EURid and DNS Belgium developed a new screening procedure to identify suspicious sites. Every new domain name is checked against a series of parameters to determine if it is suspicious. If the domain name matches several of the parameters, an 8-step verification process is triggered, which requires applicants to provide proof of identity. Activation of the site is only granted at the conclusion of the verification process. Thousands of suspicious sites are being detected annually, resulting in a significant slowing of the activities of scammers.
>
> The IOS operation has also had a large impact in other economies. Some 21,910 websites were taken down during the operation in the 15 EU member states and 12 non-EU countries taking part in the operation, and counterfeits valued at more than EUR 2.5 million were seized. In addition to Europol, Eurojust played an important role in the operation.

Memorandum of Understanding on the Sale of Counterfeit Goods on the Internet

In May 2011, major online platforms and rights holders for goods for which counterfeit and pirated versions are sold online (e.g. fast-moving consumer goods, consumer electronics, fashion and luxury goods, sports goods, films, software, games and toys) entered into a *Memorandum of Understanding on the Sale of Counterfeit Goods on the Internet* (MoU).[4] The MoU was revised and signed again in 2016, to include key performance indicators (KPIs) that are designed to track its impact and measure its success.

The purpose of this voluntary agreement is to promote good practices in the fight against the sale of counterfeit goods over the Internet and to enhance collaboration between the signatories, focusing on co-operation rather than litigation to achieve results (EC, 2020b[27]) and (EC, 2013[28]). The MoU can be considered a 'laboratory'. Reported practices could set a standard for signatory online platforms and rights owners, and may prompt stakeholders not involved in the MoU to perform better in the fight against counterfeiting at national, EU and international level. The agreement is an example of how industry self-regulation can be used to address an important policy issue, with important governmental support.

The MoU contains a series of commitments by rights holders and Internet platforms to work together to combat online counterfeiting (EC, 2016[29]).The commitments are extensive, covering i) notice and takedown procedures, ii) the proactive and preventive measures that signatories could or should take to address counterfeiting, iii) tackling repeat infringers, iv) the co-operation, including sharing of information, among signatories, v) consumer confidence, information and protection and vi) the supportive role that signatories should play with customs and other law enforcement authorities in their investigations and actions to combat counterfeiting activities.

The European Commission is not a signatory, but it plays a facilitating role, e.g. by organising the meetings and ensuring that all signatories act constructively and in good faith (EC, 2013[28]). The Commission is also responsible for preparing an annual report, if needed, on the functioning and application of the MoU. To date, three reports have been issued: a 2013 report on the initial MoU (EC, 2013[28]) and two reports on the 2016 MoU, in 2017 (EC, 2017[30]) and 2020 (EC, 2020b[27]).

The EUIPO plays an important role in KPIs and the data collection exercises: it aggregates and analyses the agreed results reported by the signatories, then sends them to the Commission and the signatories. It acts as a trusted party and ensures the confidentiality of individual submissions and a neutral, non-discriminatory evaluation process.

The agreement is not a legally binding instrument and does not create any contractual or pre-contractual obligations under any law or legal system, nor does it create any liability, rights, waiver of any rights or obligations for any parties or as releasing any parties from their legal obligations. As of 7 October 2021, there were 32 signatories to the MoU, including 15 rights holders, 9 Internet platforms, and 8 industry associations. While the number of participants has increased over time, as discussed below, there have also been few withdrawals (EC, 2020b[27]).

The majority of signatories assess their collaboration under the MoU positively, indicating that close cooperation and information exchange is key to improving the efficiency and effectiveness of their anti-counterfeiting measures. The signatories appreciate that the MoU is a good platform for exchanging information, allowing them to discuss the challenges in online counterfeiting in a regular and pragmatic manner. The initiative has also been of significant value to the Commission in carrying out its other work on anti-counterfeiting.

Legislation

Two pieces of legislation are currently being considered by the European Union in the e-commerce area: the Digital Markets Act (DMA) and the Digital Services Act (DSA).[5]

The *Digital Markets Act* (DMA) aims to ensure contestable and fair markets in the digital sector across the Union where gatekeepers are present. In particular, it aims to address unfair practices[6] and practices that could undermine the contestability of markets in the digital sector being carried out by gatekeepers and thereby enhance fair and contestable online platform environment. The gatekeepers concerned with the Digital Markets Act serve as the integral connection between online businesses and consumers in relation to provision of core platform services, such as online intermediation services, video-sharing platforms or online search engines.

The *Digital Services Act* (DSA)[7] is directed at providers of online intermediaries, including online platforms and online marketplaces, social networks, content-sharing platforms, app stores, and online travel and accommodation platforms. Importantly, some of companies concerned by the DSA could be also concerned by the DMA.

The intention of the DSA is to establish a common set of rules for actors in the online ecosystem to counter illegal content, including illegal products such as the trade in counterfeit. For example, the DSA proposal introduces a notice and action mechanism that allows user to notify the presence of an illegal product.

The proposal gives also the possibility for judicial or administrative authorities to send cross-border removal orders to providers of intermediary services.

The DSA includes also more transparency requirements for online platforms. For instance, user will have to be clearly informed whether and why they are targeted by each advertisement and who paid for the advertisement. . In addition, online marketplaces will also be obliged to gather information on traders, to enhance transparency and raise trust for consumers.

In addition, the DSA will also introduce a system of trusted entities that flag illicit content (e.g. brand owners or industry associations combatting counterfeiting) and to which platforms will have to react with priority.

EUIPO

The EUIPO has been working on a strategic project aimed at enhancing IP protection on e-commerce platforms which involves gathering information about the IP protection programs in place at different platforms, such as eBay, Amazon, Alibaba, Facebook and others. The information is being put on a single webpage to assist IP owners in navigating through the different programs, particularly with respect to the different notification mechanisms.

In addition, the EUIPO is the key actor in the implementation of the MoU on the Sale of Counterfeit Goods on the Internet (as described above).

The agency is also developing a system that will enable platform operators to identify brand owner contact points in case of different areas of IP infringement. There is also interest in developing a secure system that will allow IP owners to report information on infringement, which could then be accessed by all platform operators, thereby facilitating and enhancing the effectiveness of the information sharing.

Gathering and dissemination of knowledge on online practices infringing IPR is important part of EUIPO activity. Among others EUIPO published reports on online business models used by infringers (EUIPO 2016, EUIPO 2017, EUIPO 2019) and role of social media (EUIPO 2021a) in supporting recurrent IP infringement for physical products and digital content. Recent EUIPO reports document best practices used by platforms and domain registrars to reduce the risk of online infringement (EUIPO 2021b, EUIPO 2021c).

United Kingdom

In 2012, the United Kingdom established a strategic objective to make UK domains the safest in the world for consumers and legitimate businesses to trade. Doing so required the government to engage with domain registrars in order to move against sites selling counterfeits. This resulted in the launching of Project Ashiko where funding was provided to the London Police Intellectual Property Crime Unit (PICPU). Under the project, referrals on infringing websites generally selling fake consumer goods are submitted by brand owners, which supply evidence that goods being sold are counterfeit (Group, 2020[31]). After due diligence is undertaken by PIPCU, details are sent to Nominet, the UK registrar, which organizes the suspension of the infringing domains. The initiative resulted in 135,000 sites being taken down over seven years.

United States

The National Intellectual Property Rights Coordination Center (IPR Center) is a US Government body overseen by US Immigration and Customs Enforcement, a part of the US Department of Homeland Security (DHS). The center co-ordinates the US government's enforcement of intellectual property laws. In late 2017, the center established an E-Commerce Working Group (ECWG) with key Internet platforms.

For a variety of reasons, including competition law and trade secrets protection, various stakeholders in the e-commerce supply and distribution chains historically had not shared information on problematic sellers, shippers, freight forwarders, brokers, and other third-party intermediaries involved in counterfeit trafficking. The ECWG sought to address this by providing a platform through which the four platforms could share information, which was anonymized by the government, with each other. The presumption was that the same counterfeiters were undoubtedly acting across all the platforms, which proved to be the case, and that sharing information would help to develop better intelligence on their activities. The exercise enabled the IPR center to identify targets for civil and criminal prosecution; sharing the information with other US law enforcement bodies, such as Customs and Border Protection, was also beneficial in this regard. The focus of the group was narrow, which was reflected in the membership of the group; rights holders, for example were not included. The narrow focus is seen as an important factor in its success.

The project proved to be highly successful, demonstrating the value of a robust exchange of data in i) providing platforms with the information needed to move against bad actors and ii) providing law enforcement information for further investigation and, eventually, interdiction. The platforms are advancing this work, by selecting a third-party vendor for building a large database to facilitate further data sharing, thereby reducing the role of government in the project, in a mutually agreed manner.

In January 2020, the DHS published a report on *Combatting Trafficking in Counterfeit and Pirated Goods*, which identifies 11 immediate actions to be taken to address counterfeiting problems, including development of an Anti-Counterfeiting Consortium to Identify Online Nefarious Actors (ACTION) Plan (DHS, 2020[32]).

The ACTION Plan, which builds on the work of the ECWG, comprises the following three elements (DHS, 2020[32]):

- Sharing information within the ACTION framework on sellers, shippers, and other third-party intermediaries involved in trafficking in counterfeit and pirated goods.
- Sharing of risk automation techniques, allowing ACTION members to create and improve on proactive targeting systems that automatically monitor online platform sellers for counterfeits and pirated goods.
- In addition, ACTION members may enter non-binding memoranda of understanding (MoU) with the IPR Center, consistent with US law, to clarify the expectations and legal understanding for data sharing and coordinated IPR enforcement moving forward. Such MoUs will provide a vehicle to create a compliance scoring mechanism, as well as to delineate reasonable efforts to know the seller as well as the scope of products involved (e.g. fast-moving consumer goods, consumer electronics, fashion and luxury products, sports goods, software, and games, and toys).

The ACTION Plan is designed to strengthen information sharing between platforms, while engaging certain other e-commerce entities, including payment processors, shippers and search engines. The mechanism would also be used to communicate best practices back to the private sector, and to encourage the adoption of these practices, with the IPR Center to monitor, and report on the adoption of, and the progress and effectiveness of, these best practices. Ten practices were identified (DHS, 2020[32]):

1. *Comprehensive "terms of service" agreements.* Platforms are called on to conclude stringent terms of service agreements with vendors that provide a legal means to move against sellers of counterfeit goods
2. *Significantly enhanced vetting of third-party sellers.* Enhanced vetting would encourage platforms to require a seller to provide: sufficient identification, certification as to whether it has been banned from any major e-commerce platforms and acknowledgment that it is offering trademarked products.

3. *Limitations on high-risk products.* Protocols and procedures to place limitations on the sale of products that have a higher risk of being counterfeited or pirated and/or pose a higher risk to the public health and safety
4. *Efficient notice and takedown procedures*, including create and maintain clear, precise, and objective criteria that allow for quick and efficient notice and takedowns of infringing seller profiles and product listings
5. *Enhanced post-discovery actions*, including notification to any buyer(s) likely to have purchased the goods and notification to implicated rights holders.
6. *Indemnity requirements for foreign sellers.*
7. Clear transactions through banks that comply with US enforcement requests.
8. *Pre-sale identification of third-party sellers*, factoring in the likelihood of being sold a counterfeit or IPR infringing merchandise.
9. *Establish marketplace seller IDs*. This would improve communication to the consumer in a more holistic view of "who" is selling the goods, linking all related sellers together and enhancing internal risk assessment.
10. *Clearly identifiable country of origin disclosures.*

With respect to next steps, some social media sites with e-commerce platforms have joined the consortia, and they are receiving special attention as they seek to implement improved practices. Increased attention is now being paid with social media sites, a number of which have joined the consortia which are also operating e-commerce platforms. With the aforementioned information sharing platform close to deployment, the identification of bad actors should be greatly facilitated. Overall, the need for all stakeholders involved in e-commerce to co-operate with one another in combatting online sales of counterfeits is great and efforts to ensure this are ongoing. The progress being made on all fronts will be examined in an upcoming report that is expected to be published in the third quarter of 2021.

Legislation

Legislation is currently being considered in the United States to address a number of e-commerce issues. The Integrity, Notification, and Fairness in Online Retail Marketplaces for Consumers Act (INFORM Consumers Act) would require online marketplaces to collect, verify, and disclose certain information from high-volume, third-party sellers.[8]

Another example is the Stopping Harmful Offers on Platforms by Screening Against Fakes in E-commerce Act of 2021 (SHOP SAFE Act). The Act is going to reduce the online availability of harmful fakes through a number of mechanisms. This would give ecommerce platforms liability for counterfeit products that pose a health risk. If harmful fake products are sold on the platform, the brand owner or customer could hold the ecommerce platform liable. In addition the Act creates incentives for online platforms to establish best practices such as vetting sellers to ensure their legitimacy, removing counterfeit listings, and removing sellers who repeatedly sell counterfeits.

Actions of online platforms

Online platforms have themselves been developing policies and procedures for preventing their abuse by counterfeiters, either on their own, or in co-ordination with national authorities. Broadly speaking, these efforts and practices focused on sellers, buyers and right holders.[9]

Sellers

Actions that platforms can take and that are focus on sellers are rooted in comprehensive terms of service agreements that selling partners are obliged to agree to. Such agreements prohibit explicitly the sale of counterfeit products and they put sellers on notice of the consequences of doing so, providing the platform with a clear legal basis to take action. Such terms of service are applied by many platforms, including Amazon, Walmart or Mercado Libre. For example Amazon requires sellers that reach a specific sales level are to carry insurance to cover any potential damage caused by their products to a US consumer, regardless of where their products are manufactured.

Another seller-oriented practice concerns controls on sellers and products that can rely on algorithms, heuristics, machine learning capabilities and investigators. For example at Amazon, during registration, sellers are required to provide a government-issued photo ID and additional personal and financial information that is then verified to identify potential risks. Walmart also applies verification procedures to third party sellers prior to allowing them to operate on the platform. In addition, vetting is carried out for products prone to counterfeiting (e.g. luxury brands or electronics products) and high-risk geographic regions. Mercado Libre, an e-commerce platform founded in 1999, which now operates in 18 Latin American countries is rolling out a know-your-customer (KYC) approach. The KYC authenticates sellers on the platform, with a view towards combating all types of fraud including counterfeiting. Under the program, prospective sellers need to submit information and "proof of life" evidence that validates their identities, in order to operate on the platform. The initiative is already yielding positive results. In Brazil, for example, where there was a significant problem with the selling of counterfeit books, use of the KYC mechanism enabled the company to reduce claims from members of the program by 99%.

Consumers

Consumer-focused measures employed by platforms include in most cases additional information about sellers provided to consumers. This includes for example tools provided to sellers to share voluntarily more information about themselves and their products. It refers to such features like profile pages for sellers, store pages for brand owners and an in-house buyer-selling messaging service that allows customers to learn more about sellers and products.

Such options are provided by, for example, Amazon. Moreover, the platform informs customers whether they are buying directly from Amazon, or from a third party. In the case of the latter, seller contact information is provided on the product listing.

Brand owners

A large volume of anti-counterfeiting measures that platforms can employ is focused on brand owners, whose rights are infringed. Indeed brand owners have clear incentives to counter proactively the risk of counterfeits offered online, as for them it implies clear short and long term losses of foregone sales, deceived customers, and eroded brand.

Many of these measures are facilitated by public actors. For example the EUIPO has been working with a number of e commerce marketplaces to gather information on their IP protection tools to make it easier for relevant parties to take action and use the resources they make available.[10]

One of the fundamental measures is an efficient notification system that allow brand owners to report listings that are potentially infringing their IP rights. These systems vary across platforms and include web forms, or forms that can be downloaded and sent by email. The exact information required also varies; in most cases it includes information about company, your IP rights (e.g. trade mark registration number) and the allegedly infringing listings (e.g. URL). For example Amazon includes a notice and takedown mechanisms supported with additional scan of the platform for additional counterfeits.

Another example of an IP-right owner centred practice are IP protection programmes that are put in place by some online marketplaces to support their cooperation with IP owners. The programmes typically offer a simplified process for notice and take-down infringing listings and a dashboard to keep track of right owner's notifications and their outcomes. In addition, they can facilitate searches for counterfeit listings. For example Amazon offers the brand registry that uses machine learning to scan for potential infringements. Another example is the Verified Rights Owner partnership program (VeRO) created by eBay in 1998. The program provides a mechanism for the rights owners to report on listings that infringe on their copyright, trademark, or other intellectual property rights to eBay, which then takes action to remove the listing.

A dedicated contact point is another example of a right-owner oriented practice. The contact point offers right owners assistance in case they are facing an issue using a notification system or joining an IP protection programme. For example eBay has dedicated brand protection managers who partner with brand owners to gather intelligence that is then used proactively to detect counterfeit products.

References

Amazon (2021), *Brand Protection Report*, https://assets.aboutamazon.com/96/a0/90f229d54c8cba5072b2c4e021f7/amz-brand-report.pdf. [41]

Andrenelli, A. (2019), "Electronic transmissions and international trade - shedding new light on the moratorium debate", *OECD Trade Policy Papers*, Vol. 233, https://doi.org/10.1787/57b50a4b-en. [16]

DHS (2020), *Combating Trafficking in Counterfeit and Pirated Goods*, US Department of Homeland Security, Washington, https://www.dhs.gov/sites/default/files/publications/20_0124_plcy_counterfeit-pirated-goods-report_01.pdf. [32]

eBay (2021), *2020 Global Transparency Report*, http://www.ebaymainstreet.com/sites/default/files/2021-05/2020-eBay-Global-Transparency-Report.pdf. [40]

EC (2017), *Overview of the functioning of the Memorandum of Understanding on the sale of counterfeit goods via the internet, SWD(2017) 430 final*, https://ec.europa.eu/docsroom/documents/26602. [30]

EC (2016), *Memorandum of Understanding: 21 June 2016, Ref. Ares(2016)3934515 26/07/2016*, European Commission, Brussels, https://ec.europa.eu/docsroom/documents/43321/attachments/2/translations/en/renditions/native. [29]

EC (2013), *Report from the Commission to the European Parliament and the Council on the Functioning of the Memorandum of Understanding on the Sale of Counterfeit Goods via the Internet, COM(2013), 209 final,*, European Commission, Brussels,, http://Ref. Ares(2016). [28]

EC (2020b), *Report on the functioning of the Memorandum of Understanding on the sale of Counterfeit Goods on the internet, SWD(2020) 166 final/2*, European Commission, Brussels, https://ec.europa.eu/docsroom/documents/42701. [27]

EUIPO (2021), *Monitoring and analysing social media in relation to IPR infringement Report*, https://euipo.europa.eu/tunnel-web/secure/webdav/guest/document_library/observatory/documents/reports/2021_Monitoring_and_analysing_social_media_in_relation_to_IPR_Infringement_Report/2021_Monitoring_and_analysing_social_media_in_relation_to_IPR_Infringem. [20]

EUIPO (2021), *New and existing trends in using social media for IP infringement activities and good practices to address them*, https://euipo.europa.eu/tunnel-web/secure/webdav/guest/document_library/observatory/documents/reports/2021_Social_Media/2021_Social_Media_Discussion_Paper_FullR_en.pdf. [19]

GCIG (2016), *One Internet, Centre for International Governance Innovation and Chatham House*, http://www.cigionline.org/documents/1045/gcig_final_report_-_with_cover.pdf. [39]

Goldberg, S. (2019), "Regulating Privacy Online: An Economic Evaluation of the GDPR", *SSRN Working Paper*, http://dx.doi.org/10.2139/ssrn.3421731. [21]

Group, I. (2020), *IP Crime and Enforcement Report*, IP Crime Group Secretariat, Concept House, Newport, https://assets.publishing.service.gov.uk/government/uploads/system/uploads/attachment_data/file/913644/ip-crime-report-2019-20.pdf. [31]

INTA (2020), *Addressing the Sale of Counterfeits on the Internet*, https://www.inta.org/wp-content/uploads/public-files/advocacy/committee-reports/Addressing_the_Sale_of_Counterfeits_on_the_Internet_June_2021_edit.pdf. [22]

OCDE/EUIPO (2021), *Misuse of Containerized Maritime Shipping in the Global Trade of Counterfeits*, Éditions OCDE, Paris,, https://doi.org/10.1787/e39d8939-en. [9]

OECD (2021), *COVID-19 vaccine and the Threat of Illicit Trade, Chair's Summary Note*, https://www.oecd.org/gov/illicit-trade/summary-note-covid-19-vaccine-and-the-threat-of-illicit-trade.pdf. [35]

OECD (2021), *Illicit trade: Discussions with stakeholders*, unpublished. [26]

OECD (2020), *Illicit Trade in a Time of Crisis. Chair's Summary Note*, https://www.oecd.org/gov/illicit-trade/oecd-webinar-illicit-trade-time-crisis-23-april.pdf. [10]

OECD (2020), *OECD Digital Economy Outlook 2020*, OECD Publishing, Paris, https://doi.org/10.1787/bb167041-en. [11]

OECD (2020), *Trade in Fake Medicines at the Time of the Covid-19 Pandemics. Chair's Summary Note*, https://www.oecd.org/gov/illicit-trade/oecd-fake-medicines-webinar-june-10-summary-note.pdf. [34]

OECD (2018), *Governance Frameworks to Counter Illicit Trade*, OECD Publishing, Paris,, https://doi.org/10.1787/9789264291652-en. [33]

OECD (2011), *OECD Council Recommendation on Principles for Internet Policy Making*, OECD, Paris, https://www.oecd.org/sti/ieconomy/49258588.pdf. [37]

OECD (2008), *The Economic Impact of Counterfeiting and Piracy*, Éditions OCDE, Paris, https://doi.org/10.1787/9789264045521-en. [13]

OECD (2016a), *Ministerial Declaration on the Digital Economy*, OECD, http://www.oecd.org/digital/Digital-Economy-Ministerial-Declaration-2016.pdf. [38]

OECD (2016b), *Recommendation of the Council on Consumer Protection in E-commerce*, OECD, Paris, https://legalinstruments.oecd.org/en/instruments/OECD-LEGAL-0422. [17]

OECD/EUIPO (2021), *Global Trade in Fakes: a Worrying Threat*, OECD Publishing, https://www.oecd.org/publications/global-trade-in-fakes-74c81154-en.htm. [4]

OECD/EUIPO (2020), *Trade in Counterfeit Pharmaceutical Products*, Illicit Trade, OECD Publishing, Paris, https://dx.doi.org/10.1787/a7c7e054-en. [8]

OECD/EUIPO (2019), *Trends in Trade in Counterfeit and Pirated Goods*, OECD Publishing, Paris,, https://doi.org/10.1787/g2g9f533-en. [3]

OECD/EUIPO (2018), *Misuse of Small Parcels for Trade in Counterfeit Goods: Facts and Trends*, OECD Publishing, Paris, https://doi.org/10.1787/9789264307858-en. [7]

OECD/EUIPO (2018), *Trade in Counterfeit Goods and Free Trade Zones: Evidence from Recent Trends*, OECD Publishing, Paris/EUIPO, Alicante, https://doi.org/10.1787/9789264289550-en. [5]

OECD/EUIPO (2018), *Why Do Countries Export Fakes?: The Role of Governance Frameworks, Enforcement and Socio-economic Factors*, OECD Publishing, Paris/EUIPO, Alicante, https://doi.org/10.1787/9789264302464-en. [6]

OECD/EUIPO (2017), *Mapping the Real Routes of Trade in Fake Goods, Illicit Trade*, OECD Publishing, Paris, https://doi.org/10.1787/9789264278349-en. [2]

OECD/EUIPO (2016), *Trade in Counterfeit and Pirated Goods: Mapping the Economic Impact, Illicit Trade*, OECD Publishing, Paris, https://doi.org/10.1787/9789264252653-en. [1]

Phaneuf, A. (2021), *Social Commerce 2021: Social media and Ecommerce Convergence Trends Brings Growth Opportunity for Brands, Insider Inc.*,, http://www.businessinsider.com/social-commerce-brand-trends-marketing-strategies. [18]

S. Goldberg, G. (2019), "Regulating Privacy Online: An Economic Evaluation of the GDPR", *SSRN Working Paper*, http://dx.doi.org/10.2139/ssrn.3421731. [42]

Sorescu, S. (2021), "Trade in the time of parcels", *OECD Trade Policy Papers*, Vol. 249, https://doi.org/10.1787/0faac348-en. [15]

Tian, H. (2018), *Bullet-proof payment processors*, https://ieeexplore.ieee.org/document/8376208. [23]

UNCTAD (2021), *Estimates of global e-commerce 2019 and preliminary assessment of COVID-19 impact on online retail 2020*, United Nations Conference on Trade and Development, Geneva, https://unctad.org/system/files/official-document/tn_unctad_ict4d18_en.pdf. [14]

UNICRI (2020), *"Cyber-crime during the COVID-19 Pandemic"*, http://www.unicri.it/news/cyber-crime-during-covid-19-pandemic. [12]

UPU (2020), *E-commerce Guide*, Universal Postal Union, Berne, https://www.upu.int/UPU/media/upu/publications/Final-November-update-UPU-E-Commerce-Guide_2020_EN.pdf. [25]

USPS (2020/21), *FY 2020 Annual Report to Congress*, United States Postal Service, https://about.usps.com/what/financials/annual-reports/fy2020.pdf. [24]

WCO (2020), *Illicit Trade Report 2019*, WCO, Brussels,, http://www.wcoomd.org/-/media/wco/public/global/pdf/topics/enforcement-and-compliance/activities-and-programmes/illicit-trade-report/itr_2019_en.pdf?db=web. [36]

Notes

¹ Except as noted, the assessment is based on discussions carried out in 2021 with the countries concerned.

² See https://www.ipaustralia.gov.au/about-us.

³ See https://docs.aws.amazon.com/qldb/latest/developerguide/what-is.html.

⁴ See https://ec.europa.eu/growth/industry/policy/intellectual-property/enforcement/memorandum-understanding-sale-counterfeit-goods-internet_en.

⁵ As for September 2021.

⁶ See https://ec.europa.eu/info/strategy/priorities-2019-2024/europe-fit-digital-age/digital-markets-act-ensuring-fair-and-open-digital-markets_en#new-rules-in-a-nutshell.

⁷ See https://ec.europa.eu/commission/presscorner/detail/en/QANDA_20_2348

⁸ See www.congress.gov/bill/117th-congress/senate-bill/936.

⁹ Except as noted, the assessment is based on discussions carried out in 2021 with the companies concerned.

¹⁰ See https://euipo.europa.eu/ohimportal/en/web/observatory/e-commerce

6 Concluding remarks

E-commerce continues to expand globally, bringing significant benefits to business and consumers alike, providing them with opportunities to purchase a wide variety of goods at competitive prices. Continuous technological improvements that facilitate e-commerce reduce transaction costs, and provide more information to participants, boosting access to a wider array of products, leading to efficiency gains, as well as resulting in welfare improvements for the entire economy. Of particular interest is the expansion of traditional brick and mortar establishments into e-commerce. It is affecting an ever-expanding number of companies across virtually all business segments. Small businesses are taking advantage; small local proprietors are, for example, providing consumers with possibilities to order and pay for merchandise, for pick up or delivery, replacing more cumbersome transactions carried out by phone, or through physical visits to the businesses concerned.

The COVID-19 crisis accelerated an expansion of e-commerce towards new firms, customers and types of products. It has provided consumers with access to a significant variety of products from the convenience and safety of their homes, and has enabled firms to continue operation in spite of contact restrictions and other confinement measures.

At the same time, the online environment has become more intensely misused, and cyber law enforcement has reported skyrocketing volumes of various e-crimes. E-commerce is becoming an important platform for illicit products, including fake and substandard medicines, test kits and other COVID-19-related goods.

The explosive growth in e-commerce is paralleled an unprecedented increase in growth in small shipments, handled primarily through postal services.

For criminals running illicit trade networks, small parcels sent by post become an attractive way of fulfilment of on-line transaction. In addition, small shipments provide a means for counterfeiters to lower the potential losses that result from seizures. This is confirmed by observable trends. While counterfeits trafficked by container ships clearly dominate in terms of value, trafficking of fakes by small parcels, sent mostly by post, is growing and dominate in terms of number of seizures.

The quantitative analysis provided in this report employs large datasets to provide more detailed and precise information about the quantitative relationship between illicit trade in counterfeits and the indicators on e-commerce.

The analysis confirms a positive and statistically significant correlation between the indicators of e-commerce activity in an economy, and imports of counterfeits to that economy. This analysis re-confirms the intuitive claim that for criminals, e-commerce provides an increasingly attractive means to facilitate the trade in counterfeit goods for a large range of product categories.

Furthermore, the correlation becomes stronger for indicators of imports of fakes with small parcels. Countries that report high degrees of e-commerce intensity (approximated by all available indicators) tend to report higher rates of imports of fakes smuggled in small parcels. Although indirectly, it re-confirms another intuitive observation that small parcels are the preferred way of shipping of fake products ordered via e-commerce.

The subsequent analysis focused on the imports of fakes to the EU, taking into account additional information provided in the EU data.

Overall the conclusion was that a majority of seizures of goods imported to the EU from third countries refer to goods that have been purchased on-line. However, in terms of their value, only 14% of value of counterfeit goods imported to the EU referred to goods purchased on-line. Limitations of data do not allow to assess the scale of e-commerce solutions employed to sell fakes in transactions carried out entirely within the EU borders. But both the statistics indicating rapid growth of e-commerce in recent years in general and the fact that only a fraction of e-commerce B2C transactions are performed cross border indicate that the real role of e-commerce in trade in counterfeit could be considerably more important than indicated in the present study.

In terms of provenance economies, China and Hong-Kong (China) were the source of over 80% of detentions with a link to online sale, in terms of both: seizures and values.

Regarding transport modes, small parcels were the main method of transport of fakes ordered on-line to the EU. A closer look into specific streams reveals that the postal distribution channel clearly dominated. Over 90% of seizures of fakes ordered on-line were carried by post.

In terms of products, many types of fake products tend to be ordered on-line including footwear, clothes, toys, leather goods, electric equipment and watches and cosmetics. The two rankings – in terms of value and number of seizures -- are quite similar, with footwear and clothing being product categories on top of the list of products with highest shares of detentions.

The quantitative analysis presented identifies several research areas that might merit further investigation. A more in-depth analysis of these topics could be beneficial for developing efficient enforcement and governance frameworks to counter the risks posed by trade in counterfeit goods ordered on-line.

Existing qualitative information highlight that the on-line market for misuse of small parcels is very dynamic. In addition, the COVID-19 pandemic has added lots of momentum. Further investigation into how these dynamics evolve is needed – either at the industry level or through a case-by-case analysis. This investigation could take into account more nuanced aspects of the dynamic changes in industry/economy structure of use of the on-line environment.

Policy makers and the private sector are concerned about the significant scope of counterfeit trade abusing e-commerce to harm legitimate businesses and economic activity, and to cause damage to the health, safety and security of citizens. Existing legislative in the e-commerce area are being considered in the European Union and in the United States. The Digital Services Act in the EU and the SHOP SAFE Act in the US are directed at online intermediaries and platforms. They will establish a common set of rules for actors in the online ecosystem, and diminish the volume of fakes available online. It will be done through a number of mechanisms, the key one being streamlining of ecommerce platforms liability for counterfeit products, in particular those that pose health and safety risks.

The analysis presented in this report could be used to strengthen development and implementation of such actions, and to further effective cooperation between customs authorities, postal and express operators, e-commerce platforms and right holders, in particular by improving mechanisms for collecting and sharing good quality information.

References

Amazon (2021), *Brand Protection Report*, https://assets.aboutamazon.com/96/a0/90f229d54c8cba5072b2c4e021f7/amz-brand-report.pdf. [41]

Andrenelli, A. (2019), "Electronic transmissions and international trade - shedding new light on the moratorium debate", *OECD Trade Policy Papers*, Vol. 233, https://doi.org/10.1787/57b50a4b-en. [16]

DHS (2020), *Combating Trafficking in Counterfeit and Pirated Goods*, US Department of Homeland Security, Washington, https://www.dhs.gov/sites/default/files/publications/20_0124_plcy_counterfeit-pirated-goods-report_01.pdf. [32]

eBay (2021), *2020 Global Transparency Report*, http://www.ebaymainstreet.com/sites/default/files/2021-05/2020-eBay-Global-Transparency-Report.pdf. [40]

EC (2017), *Overview of the functioning of the Memorandum of Understanding on the sale of counterfeit goods via the internet, SWD(2017) 430 final*, https://ec.europa.eu/docsroom/documents/26602. [30]

EC (2016), *Memorandum of Understanding: 21 June 2016, Ref. Ares(2016)3934515 26/07/2016*, European Commission, Brussels, https://ec.europa.eu/docsroom/documents/43321/attachments/2/translations/en/renditions/native. [29]

EC (2013), *Report from the Commission to the European Parliament and the Council on the Functioning of the Memorandum of Understanding on the Sale of Counterfeit Goods via the Internet, COM(2013), 209 final,*, European Commission, Brussels,, http://Ref. Ares(2016). [28]

EC (2020b), *Report on the functioning of the Memorandum of Understanding on the sale of Counterfeit Goods on the internet, SWD(2020) 166 final/2*, European Commission, Brussels, https://ec.europa.eu/docsroom/documents/42701. [27]

EUIPO (2021), *Monitoring and analysing social media in relation to IPR infringement Report*, https://euipo.europa.eu/tunnel-web/secure/webdav/guest/document_library/observatory/documents/reports/2021_Monitoring_and_analysing_social_media_in_relation_to_IPR_Infringement_Report/2021_Monitoring_and_analysing_social_media_in_relation_to_IPR_Infringem. [20]

EUIPO (2021), *New and existing trends in using social media for IP infringement activities and good practices to address them*, https://euipo.europa.eu/tunnel-web/secure/webdav/guest/document_library/observatory/documents/reports/2021_Social_Media/2021_Social_Media_Discussion_Paper_FullR_en.pdf. [19]

GCIG (2016), *One Internet, Centre for International Governance Innovation and Chatham House*, http://www.cigionline.org/documents/1045/gcig_final_report_-_with_cover.pdf. [39]

Goldberg, S. (2019), "Regulating Privacy Online: An Economic Evaluation of the GDPR", *SSRN Working Paper*, http://dx.doi.org/10.2139/ssrn.3421731. [21]

Group, I. (2020), *IP Crime and Enforcement Report*, IP Crime Group Secretariat, Concept House, Newport, https://assets.publishing.service.gov.uk/government/uploads/system/uploads/attachment_data/file/913644/ip-crime-report-2019-20.pdf. [31]

INTA (2020), *Addressing the Sale of Counterfeits on the Internet*, https://www.inta.org/wp-content/uploads/public-files/advocacy/committee-reports/Addressing_the_Sale_of_Counterfeits_on_the_Internet_June_2021_edit.pdf. [22]

OCDE/EUIPO (2021), *Misuse of Containerized Maritime Shipping in the Global Trade of Counterfeits*, Éditions OCDE, Paris,, https://doi.org/10.1787/e39d8939-en. [9]

OECD (2021), *COVID-19 vaccine and the Threat of Illicit Trade, Chair's Summary Note*, https://www.oecd.org/gov/illicit-trade/summary-note-covid-19-vaccine-and-the-threat-of-illicit-trade.pdf. [35]

OECD (2021), *Illicit trade: Discussions with stakeholders*, unpublished. [26]

OECD (2020), *Illicit Trade in a Time of Crisis. Chair's Summary Note*, https://www.oecd.org/gov/illicit-trade/oecd-webinar-illicit-trade-time-crisis-23-april.pdf. [10]

OECD (2020), *OECD Digital Economy Outlook 2020*, OECD Publishing, Paris, https://doi.org/10.1787/bb167041-en. [11]

OECD (2020), *Trade in Fake Medicines at the Time of the Covid-19 Pandemics. Chair's Summary Note*, https://www.oecd.org/gov/illicit-trade/oecd-fake-medicines-webinar-june-10-summary-note.pdf. [34]

OECD (2018), *Governance Frameworks to Counter Illicit Trade*, OECD Publishing, Paris,, https://doi.org/10.1787/9789264291652-en. [33]

OECD (2011), *OECD Council Recommendation on Principles for Internet Policy Making*, OECD, Paris, https://www.oecd.org/sti/ieconomy/49258588.pdf. [37]

OECD (2008), *The Economic Impact of Counterfeiting and Piracy*, Éditions OCDE, Paris, https://doi.org/10.1787/9789264045521-en. [13]

OECD (2016a), *Ministerial Declaration on the Digital Economy*, OECD, http://www.oecd.org/digital/Digital-Economy-Ministerial-Declaration-2016.pdf. [38]

OECD (2016b), *Recommendation of the Council on Consumer Protection in E-commerce*, OECD, Paris, https://legalinstruments.oecd.org/en/instruments/OECD-LEGAL-0422. [17]

OECD/EUIPO (2021), *Global Trade in Fakes: a Worrying Threat*, OECD Publishing, https://www.oecd.org/publications/global-trade-in-fakes-74c81154-en.htm. [4]

OECD/EUIPO (2020), *Trade in Counterfeit Pharmaceutical Products*, Illicit Trade, OECD Publishing, Paris, https://dx.doi.org/10.1787/a7c7e054-en. [8]

OECD/EUIPO (2019), *Trends in Trade in Counterfeit and Pirated Goods*, OECD Publishing, Paris,, https://doi.org/10.1787/g2g9f533-en. [3]

OECD/EUIPO (2018), *Misuse of Small Parcels for Trade in Counterfeit Goods: Facts and Trends*, OECD Publishing, Paris, https://doi.org/10.1787/9789264307858-en. [7]

OECD/EUIPO (2018), *Trade in Counterfeit Goods and Free Trade Zones: Evidence from Recent Trends*, OECD Publishing, Paris/EUIPO, Alicante, https://doi.org/10.1787/9789264289550-en. [5]

OECD/EUIPO (2018), *Why Do Countries Export Fakes?: The Role of Governance Frameworks, Enforcement and Socio-economic Factors*, OECD Publishing, Paris/EUIPO, Alicante, https://doi.org/10.1787/9789264302464-en. [6]

OECD/EUIPO (2017), *Mapping the Real Routes of Trade in Fake Goods, Illicit Trade*, OECD Publishing, Paris, https://doi.org/10.1787/9789264278349-en. [2]

OECD/EUIPO (2016), *Trade in Counterfeit and Pirated Goods: Mapping the Economic Impact, Illicit Trade*, OECD Publishing, Paris, https://doi.org/10.1787/9789264252653-en. [1]

Phaneuf, A. (2021), *Social Commerce 2021: Social media and Ecommerce Convergence Trends Brings Growth Opportunity for Brands, Insider Inc.,*, http://www.businessinsider.com/social-commerce-brand-trends-marketing-strategies. [18]

S. Goldberg, G. (2019), "Regulating Privacy Online: An Economic Evaluation of the GDPR", *SSRN Working Paper*, http://dx.doi.org/10.2139/ssrn.3421731. [42]

Sorescu, S. (2021), "Trade in the time of parcels", *OECD Trade Policy Papers*, Vol. 249, https://doi.org/10.1787/0faac348-en. [15]

Tian, H. (2018), *Bullet-proof payment processors*, https://ieeexplore.ieee.org/document/8376208. [23]

UNCTAD (2021), *Estimates of global e-commerce 2019 and preliminary assessment of COVID-19 impact on online retail 2020*, United Nations Conference on Trade and Development, Geneva, https://unctad.org/system/files/official-document/tn_unctad_ict4d18_en.pdf. [14]

UNICRI (2020), *"Cyber-crime during the COVID-19 Pandemic"*, http://www.unicri.it/news/cyber-crime-during-covid-19-pandemic. [12]

UPU (2020), *E-commerce Guide*, Universal Postal Union, Berne, https://www.upu.int/UPU/media/upu/publications/Final-November-update-UPU-E-Commerce-Guide_2020_EN.pdf. [25]

USPS (2020/21), *FY 2020 Annual Report to Congress*, United States Postal Service, https://about.usps.com/what/financials/annual-reports/fy2020.pdf. [24]

WCO (2020), *Illicit Trade Report 2019*, WCO, Brussels,, http://www.wcoomd.org/-/media/wco/public/global/pdf/topics/enforcement-and-compliance/activities-and-programmes/illicit-trade-report/itr_2019_en.pdf?db=web. [36]

www.ingramcontent.com/pod-product-compliance
Ingram Content Group UK Ltd.
Pitfield, Milton Keynes, MK11 3LW, UK
UKHW050412240426
12048UKWH00020B/1476